"Skilled in both colourful reportage and sustaining a good argument, [Saunders] provides a badly needed progressive and optimistic narrative about our future. . . . This may be the best popular book on cities since Jane Jacobs's *The Death and Life of Great American Cities*. . . . Few books can make rationalists feel optimistic and empowered for the future. [*Arrival City*] does."

—*The Guardian* (London)

"Saunders's approach is through anecdotes and vignettes, but . . . they cumulate into a persuasive whole. . . . Saunders's practical suggestions for helping immigrants . . . are sure to attract attention. . . . [A] highly readable book."   —*Financial Times*

"A masterpiece of reporting, one of the most valuable and lucid works on public policy published anywhere in years."

—*Edmonton Journal*

"Important. . . . Saunders's greatest strength lies in the global breadth of his reportage. . . . His evocative descriptions . . . transform a complex, serious subject into a page-turning read." —*Literary Review*

"A broadly researched, passionate and portentous call for a new way to look at the experience of migrants. It is essential reading . . . for all who look at the future of cities with a mix of hope and fear."

—*Winnipeg Free Press*

"[An] incisive study of worldwide rural-to-urban migration, its complex social mechanisms and the consequences of institutional neglect. . . . An essential work for those who pay attention to the effects of globalization—which is, or at least should be, nearly everyone."   —*Kirkus Reviews*

DOUG SAUNDERS

THE MYTH OF THE
MUSLIM TIDE

Doug Saunders is the European bureau chief of
The Globe and Mail. He is the author of *Arrival City*,
which won or was a finalist for several prizes and was
published in eight languages around the world.

www.dougsaunders.net

ALSO BY DOUG SAUNDERS

Arrival City

DOUG SAUNDERS

THE MYTH OF THE
MUSLIM
TIDE

DO IMMIGRANTS THREATEN
THE WEST?

VINTAGE BOOKS
A DIVISION OF RANDOM HOUSE, INC. | NEW YORK

FIRST VINTAGE BOOKS EDITION, AUGUST 2012

Copyright © 2012 by Doug Saunders

All rights reserved. Published in the United States
by Vintage Books, a division of Random House, Inc., New York, and
simultaneously in hardcover in Canada by Alfred A. Knopf Canada,
a division of Random House of Canada Limited, Toronto.

Vintage and colophon are registered trademarks of Random House, Inc.

The Cataloging-in-Publication Data for *The Myth of the Muslim Tide*
is available at the Library of Congress.

Vintage ISBN: 978-0-307-95117-5

Book design by Andrew Roberts
Cover design by Cardon Webb
Cover photographs: (top) © Jacob Silberberg/Panos Pictures;
(middle) © Jeremy Graham/dbimages/Alamy;
(bottom) © Alexandra Avakian/Contact Press Images

www.vintagebooks.com

Printed in the United States of America
10   9   8   7   6   5   4   3   2   1

CONTENTS

Open your ears; for which of you will stop
The vent of hearing when loud Rumour speaks?
I, from the Orient to the drooping West,
Making the wind my post-horse, still unfold
The acts commenced on this ball of earth:
Upon my tongues continual slanders ride,
The which in every language I pronounce,
Stuffing the ears of men with false reports.
I speak of peace, while covert enmity
Under the smile of safety wounds the world,
. . . Rumour is a pipe
Blown by surmises, jealousies, conjectures,
And of so easy and so plain a stop
That the blunt monster with uncounted heads,
The still-discordant wavering multitude,
Can play upon it.

King Henry IV, Part II

ONE
POPULAR FICTION

1 THE NEW NEIGHBOURS

ABOUT FIFTEEN YEARS AGO, my London neighbour-hood began to change. We noticed it first among the crowds on our rough-and-tumble shopping street, Holloway Road, where there were suddenly a lot more women with covered heads: some wore a colourful hijab, others the white veil popular among East Africans, still others the heavy black chador, and occasionally by the bus shelter a pair of eyes would peer from a narrow slit in the all-concealing black sack of a Saudi-style abaya and niqab. Whatever their headdress, these women tended to have a lot of children with them.

Then the street itself changed: its procession of pubs and corner stores was joined by a great many Turkish eateries, some of them excellent, along with several grotty Internet cafés and money-transfer shops with opaque Arabic signs. Within a few years, it felt as if Islam was closing in. Our after-school babysitter, a French girl who grew up in an Alpine village and was partial to all-night raves, abruptly converted to the faith of her new Algerian friends and took to cover-ing her head and praying five times a day. It made her more punctual and orderly and no less attentive to our kids, but also more sombre and less willing to eat our food.

The new immigrants from East Africa, Turkey, the Middle East and the Indian subcontinent became our friends, shopkeepers, class-mates and doctors. But it was hard, in those tense years that began this century, to avoid associating their religion with violence and extremism. Our nearest Muslim house of worship, the Finsbury Park mosque, was often visited by police; in 1997 it had been taken over by an Egyptian-born former Afghan mujahedeen fighter who called himself Abu Hamza. This hook-handed, half-blind cleric, known in tabloid headlines as "hooky mullah," delivered astringent sermons calling for the murder of non-Muslims in Islamic lands and made headlines by praising the September 11 hijackers; he was arrested and imprisoned in 2004 on terrorism and race-hatred charges. After that, the extremists were banished from the mosque and deported, its new imam was moderate, and fewer intense, bearded men hung out on the streets around it. But the sense of insecurity and tension continued, especially after a neighbour lost both her legs in the July 7, 2005, suicide-bombing attacks on the London transit system, which were committed mainly by British-born Muslims from Leeds who didn't seem all that different from some of our neighbours.

Who wouldn't worry? Even as my children befriended the Usamas and Leilas around them, I couldn't avoid glancing distrustfully at some of my new neighbours. I have lived most of my life among immigrants, and of course I am one myself, but in those dark years after the terror attacks, it was hard to avoid the sense that Muslims were different: less likely to fit in, more prone to extremism, more likely to follow the teachings of their religion than the laws and social codes of the land around them. They had big families, it seemed, and we had small ones. At times I did fear that they would become a majority, and that the illiberal beliefs of the more devout among them would become dominant, turning our taste for tolerance, sexual equality and secularism into a historical footnote. If I was capable of feeling this way, as a writer with years of experience in Muslim cultures, there must be millions of people with similar suspicions.

WE'VE BEEN HERE BEFORE. If I had lived at this same London address a dozen decades earlier, I would have watched with alarm as the pavements of Holloway Road filled with poor, oddly dressed men and with women wearing identity-concealing head-scarves. Their families segregated themselves from the native-born population, adhered to religious and political beliefs that were at odds with the dominant culture, kept customs and traditions that seemed centuries behind the times, and expanded their numbers at an astonishing rate. At that point they were using the neighbourhood as a base to plot a wave of terrorist attacks that, by the end of the 1880s, had killed more people and caused more political alarm than the jihadist attacks that began the twenty-first century would. Government reports and bestselling books of the time announced that this group was impossible to integrate into the population and would be a growing threat.

Yet in fewer than two generations, these same Irish Catholic immigrants had become fully woven into the cultural life of my neighbourhood, their distinct qualities visible in their churches and pubs but now regarded as an enhancement rather than a threat. We have forgotten how alarming the waves of Roman Catholic and Jewish immigrants from the fringes of Europe appeared to North Americans and Western Europeans only a few decades ago. Their home countries seemed less democratic, less economically free, more prone to religious law and political extremism. Right up through the early 1950s, it was commonplace for thinkers across the political spectrum to argue that Catholic immigrants were driven by the dictates of their faith to promote fascism, violence and religious extremism (for this was the condition of most of their home countries and the apparent fate of many of their diasporas) and therefore could not be assimilated into non-Catholic cultures. Until the Second World War, it had been considered reasonable in many circles to hold similar views, involving communism and crime, about Ashkenazic Jewish immigrants from Eastern Europe.

By the end of the twentieth century, though, most people had forgotten about their earlier fears of religious minorities. We lived through a period of comparative tolerance when the religious fears of the mass-immigration era were replaced with the ideological fears of the Cold War. The children of Catholic and Jewish immigrants were no longer associated in the mainstream public imagination with violence and cultural usurpation, and had become our friends, neighbours, colleagues and sometimes political leaders.

And then, in the decade after the September 11 attacks, a seemingly new argument began to appear, first in the far reaches of the Internet and the mutterings of the political right, then in increasingly mainstream and mass-market venues. It began by bolstering our suspicions of those new headscarf-wearing neighbours with a few alarming anecdotes, then fanned them into smouldering distrust with some demographic and statistical claims and a bit of theology, and finally drew them to an explosive conclusion about the fate of Western societies. This argument became the subject of dozens of bestselling books, opinion pieces, blog postings, YouTube videos, political party platforms and campaign speeches, and by now has become an almost common-sense assumption for many people.

It goes like this. These Muslim immigrants, and their children and grandchildren, are not like earlier groups. They are reproducing at an unusually rapid pace, with fertility rates far higher than those of exhausted Western populations, and at some point soon—perhaps by mid-century—Muslims will become a majority in European countries and North American cities. This is a danger because, unlike other immigrants, they are loyal to Islam, not to their host society. They do not regard their religion as a private source of inspiration, but as a political ideology they intend to act upon. A line of shared belief connects the moderate Muslim believer to the radical Islamist and makes the majority of Muslims impossible to assimilate. They will permanently alter the West and promote a political agenda that will destroy our traditions and freedoms. In short, we are about to be swept away by a "Muslim tide."

THE PURPOSE OF THIS BOOK is to show that all of those claims are demonstrably untrue, and are based on the same mixture of honest misunderstandings and darker fallacies that greeted earlier waves of poor immigrants from different religious cultures. I have drawn on the most comprehensive demographic, statistical, scholarly and survey data available to provide a detailed, honest, point-by-point examination of the facts about Muslim immigrants in the West: their population growth rates; their loyalties; their religious, political and cultural behaviours and beliefs; their propensity to religious fundamentalism, to political extremism and to violence; their successes and, sometimes, their failings in becoming integrated into the economies and cultures of the West.

The stakes here are high. The Muslim-tide beliefs have already become the founding myth behind several alarming political movements and the cause of one notable act of terrorism. Promoting these myths about Muslim immigrants has become a significant mainstream theme in the electoral politics of the United States, Germany, France, the Netherlands and Scandinavia, with scarcely any proper fact checking of the underlying claims. Once again, a fever is infecting the minds of many Westerners. We must not allow history to repeat itself.

THIS BOOK IS NOT a defence of Islam, and does not contain a dissection of the teachings of the Koran. I am not an admirer of Islam, or a religious person of any sort. I am deeply alarmed by any prospect of a greater religious role in the public sphere. I am in agreement with secular Muslims such as Ayaan Hirsi Ali, Salman Rushdie, Mona Eltahawy and Fadela Amara when they argue that the instructions of the Koran and the cultural practices of many Muslim countries are enormously harmful to those who are subject to them, especially women. My view, however, is that the solution lies in the economic and political development of immigrant communities, as it has with earlier conservative religious minorities. I do not dismiss the Muslim-tide arguments out of hand. If there were evidence that their larger claims were true, I would be genuinely worried.

Theology is not the issue here, but rather public and political behaviour. The arguments for and against the Muslim-tide hypothesis are too often built on the more alarming scriptural passages of the Koran and its later, severe interpretations, or on the menacing words of certain imams and mullahs. The truth about Muslim communities is found not in scripture but in action. The holy books of every Abrahamic religion contain plenty of fodder for extremist sectarianism and for holy violence; the question is whether these words are being followed by immigrants in the West and their descendants.

We need to put aside the theology and ask a set of concrete questions: To what extent are these immigrants religiously observant or literalist believers? What role do they believe religion should play in politics? To what extent do their children and grandchildren carry the beliefs, and degrees of observance, of their parents? Where do these communities' loyalties lie? Where are their sources of self-identity?

This book is also not intended to play down the significance of the dangerous political, militant and terrorist movements that have exploded within some Muslim communities in recent decades. Rather, I hope to show that these movements are distinct and troubling products of particular political circumstances—not inevitable, organic outgrowths of conventional Islamic culture, any more than terrorist and religious extremist movements in Western cultures have been extensions of everyday thought. My work and my life have brought me too close to this violence to dismiss it. I was living in the United States during the September 11, 2001, attacks and in London during the July 7, 2005, attacks, and I was in southern France during the killing spree committed by Mohamed Merah in Toulouse in March 2012.

I have reported in depth on Islamic extremism—and moderation—from Iran, Turkey, Egypt, Libya, Tunisia, Syria, Afghanistan, Bangladesh and India, and from the capitals of Europe and North America, and as a result I do not believe that the war on terror was ill-founded or misconceived. All is not well in Muslim communities. By demonstrating in these pages that recent Muslim immigrants are no more threatening than earlier waves of poor newcomers, I hope to show them as fellow citizens whose children face specific threats that deserve attention and help. It is vitally important to separate the real problems with Muslim immigration from those that are manufactured out of fear and bad information. The idea of a stealth takeover by Islamic believers is a delusion. So is the more moderate idea of a permanently alien and impossible-to-integrate "civilization" in our midst. Real problems, as worrying to the majority of Muslims as they are to the rest of us, include the rise of anti-Semitism among the children of immigrants who identify with a mythic and faraway Middle East; a set of backward-looking subcultures that treat women as lesser beings, even possessions, to be guarded, hidden or abused; and the defensive retreat of the embittered few into all-consuming religious faith in an otherwise fast-secularizing diaspora.

These reactions, along with the remaining instances of violent Islamic extremism, are best understood as intense responses by insecure people to the modernizing trends of individualism and globalization—the very same trends that produced the Muslim-tide theories and political movements in the West. These are clashes *within* civilizations, not between them, and to a large extent they are products of the false belief, held by Muslims and non-Muslims alike, that the world is divided into fixed and irreconcilable civilizations. The larger threat comes not from these immigrants themselves, but from our response to them.

II CRESCENT FEVER
THE BRIEF HISTORY OF AN IDEA

SHORTLY AFTER LUNCHTIME, Anders Behring Breivik logged on to his computer, inserted a memory stick, and pulled up the Microsoft Word document he had finished formatting late the previous night. On this warm holiday Friday in 2011, he felt a sense of exalted relief. After he'd spent three years writing, first at his mother's home and then at the farmhouse he'd rented for his project, it ran to 1,518 densely typed pages, with a stark red Templar cross on the cover. He scrolled to page 1472, typed "I believe this will be my last entry. It is now Fri July 22nd, 12:51," signed it, sent it to a mailing list made up mainly of his Facebook friends, and logged off for the last time.

He then changed into the figure-hugging Lycra police uniform he had fabricated with obsessive delight, prepared his weapons, climbed into a Volkswagen van he had rented from Avis, and drove carefully to Oslo's central government building. The security guards, noticing the police uniform, paid little attention to the cube van as it parked in the front courtyard. Breivik took five minutes to walk several blocks away from the vehicle before the fuse ignited the detonator. When the blast wave reached him he did not turn or hesitate, but walked quickly to a Fiat van he had parked downtown the day before and began the drive to the fjord island of Utøya. As he drove westward, scores of emergency and police vehicles raced past him in the opposite direction, scrambling to deal with the deaths, grievous injuries and collapsing wreckage caused by the bomb. It was the height of the summer holidays, during which most Norwegians vacate the city, so Breivik knew the emergency services would be understaffed and unable to deal quickly with any other crises. That was part of the plan.

Aboard the ferry to Utøya an hour later, he flashed a forged police badge and explained that he had been sent to the island to counsel the teens and young adults gathered at the governing Labour Party's summer camp about the tragedy that had just occurred in Oslo. Many of the kids had family and friends employed in the government building, so it seemed a plausible explanation, even if there was something excessively flamboyant about his uniform and overexcited in his demeanour.

Breivik stepped onto the tiny island and marched decisively through the light drizzle toward the clubhouse where two hundred kids were sitting out the rain. From the front lawn, he yelled, "Everyone gather around, I have an important message about the bomb attack earlier today." As they stepped onto the lawn to meet him, he opened fire, first shooting the 45-year-old mother of two who had showed him the way from the ferry landing to the clubhouse, then dozens of young campers. As the children fled back into the building, he threw smoke bombs inside to drive them out again, and continued shooting. He then walked around the building into the campsite, methodically unzipping the tents and shooting any youngsters he found cowering inside. He continued to the path that followed the coast on the opposite end of the island, shooting into crowds of fleeing kids. Many threw themselves off the cliffs to escape, some plunging into the icy water and swimming or hiding in caves, others getting crushed on the rocks. He fired an automatic rifle into the water to kill fleeing swimmers, and hunted down teenagers hiding on the shore. At one point, a group of teens ran toward him, thinking a policeman had arrived to rescue them from the shooter. He gunned them down as their friends watched in horror from hiding places.

Breivik's massacre continued for nearly 90 minutes before he got through by cellphone to the police emergency line and announced his surrender. In the end, 69 people died on the island, some as young as 14. Another 8 were killed by the Oslo bomb. More than 150 were seriously injured.

Hours after the world learned of the attack, people began to circulate copies of Breivik's 1,518-page document. I received mine from a member of his Facebook list as I arrived in Oslo. Like many, I was at first confused by its title, *2083: A European Declaration of Independence*.[1] I had to wade through hundreds of pages to find its significance at last explained in precise detail. Breivik shared the popular misconception that Muslims will become a majority of Europe's population, and claimed that this threshold would be reached around 2080. At that point, he argued, they will naturally want to impose their governing ideals, in harmony with their religious instructions, and subjugate the continent's Christians and Jews. As it happens, 2083 is the four hundredth anniversary of the Battle of Vienna, when the advance of the Muslim Ottoman Empire toward the centre of Europe was stopped by the Habsburg armies. Breivik's manifesto argued that Europe is now facing a similar onslaught, and called for a repeat of that battle.

In Breivik's vision, his Oslo attacks were the opening salvo of this larger war, a cod-Wagnerian call to arms for fellow fighters against the enablers of "Eurabia." His targets, chosen to have the maximum impact in stopping the Muslim onslaught, were what he called "category A and B traitors": the politicians who were allowing and encouraging Muslim immigration, and the "suicidal humanists" and "capitalist globalists" who were tolerating the presence of Muslims within Europe. By killing the Labour Party youth, he hoped to eliminate a generation of tolerant politicians. (In fact, Norway has one of Europe's tougher immigration policies, and also one of Europe's smallest Muslim communities).

Toward the end of his document, Breivik provided the text of his proposed legal defence. "The individuals I have been accused of illegally executing are all category A and B traitors," he wrote. "They are supporters of the anti-European hate ideology known as multiculturalism, an ideology that facilitates Islamisation and Islamic demographic warfare. The category A and B traitors I executed were killed in self defence through a pre-emptive strike. They have been found guilty of high treason and condemned to death. . . . I must be allowed to prove that I executed these traitors in order to prevent them from continuing to contribute in the ongoing processes of cultural and demographical genocide and extermination."

That was outlandish stuff. Yet much of the document, once you clawed your way past its lush faux-medieval adornments, seemed strikingly sane and unnervingly familiar. True, the violent language and his invocation of a new Knights Templar army in the concluding sections were hallmarks of deep extremism and possibly insanity. But along the way to that leap of criminal absurdity, he had followed a line of reasoning that, by 2011, had become mainstream—a set of arguments that had been playing out on the bestseller charts, blog sites, opinion pages and 24-hour news networks of Europe and North America for a decade at least. Indeed, the core of his manifesto is a very long pastiche of passages from books, newspaper columns and blog posts by writers who are well-known media figures in Britain, Germany, the Netherlands, Canada and the United States. He did not develop a new argument at all, but merely cut and pasted theirs, unaltered, and appended his own violent conclusion.

Here, in this manuscript composed by a terrorist, was the history of an idea. In these pages, the notion of the Muslim tide could be traced from its emergence in fringe publications in the final decades of the twentieth century, through its rise in increasingly less obscure books and films throughout the opening decade of this one, and then into the central corridors of European and American politics. During that paranoid decade, a set of fringe concepts, built on misreadings and falsehoods, came to be embraced by a large group of writers and political leaders who should have known better.

The Outraged Moderate

Take, for example, the American writer Bruce Bawer, one of the more frequently quoted authors in Breivik's manifesto, his books lauded by the killer as important inspirations. Far from being a career racist or fringe politician, Bawer was known for nearly three decades as a gifted essayist on poetry, fiction and cinema, his subtle works on John Fowles's novels or David Lynch's screenplays published regularly in such mainstream conservative magazines as the *New Criterion* and the *American Spectator*. His first major book, *A Place at the Table: The Gay Individual in American Society*, was a defence of gay rights and same-sex marriage from a politically centrist perspective. His second, *Stealing Jesus: How Fundamentalism Betrays Christianity*, was a moderate, gay Christian's attack on evangelical excesses, in which he argued that his non-fundamentalist middle-of-the-road faith was the "true Christianity," not the angry extremism of US televangelists. [2]

Bawer had moved to Amsterdam in 1999 (and would be living in Oslo by the time of Breivik's attack). Something happened to him in the wake of 9/11. By Bawer's own account, he was shocked into consciousness living as a gay man in Amsterdam and experiencing the homophobic and antiliberal voices of the more extreme Muslim clerics after the September 11 attacks. In *While Europe Slept: How Radical Islam Is Destroying the West from Within* and other books, he repeatedly and hyperbolically described the extremist fringe of Islam as being its true (and, generally, only) aspect. His books were well received in the United States and were excerpted and praised in such mainstream outlets as the *Wall Street Journal* editorial page and

Fox News. In the final chapter of *While Europe Slept*, titled "Europe's Weimar Moment," he likens Europe today to Germany during the ascent of Hitler, with Muslims taking the place of Nazis, arriving at the inevitable conclusion: "It's hard to imagine that Americans could do much to rescue Europe from its present fate, short of launching another D-Day." In a January 2007 blog post, Bawer took this line of reasoning even further, with words that would become his most famous: "European officials have a clear route out of this nightmare" of Muslim hegemony, he wrote. "They have armies. They have police. They have prisons."

Bawer was outraged by Breivik's attack, but not simply because it was a grotesque atrocity. In his view, the killings had also brought dishonour on an important movement. "When it emerged that these acts of terror were the work of a native Norwegian who thought he was striking a blow against jihadism and its enablers," Bawer wrote in the *Wall Street Journal* two days after the killings, "it was immediately clear to me that his violence will deal a heavy blow to an urgent cause." Even as bodies were still being pulled from the Norwegian lake, he used the occasion to endorse the arguments in the *2083* manifesto. "The first half, in which [Breivik] indicts the European cultural elite for permitting Islam to take root in Europe, makes it clear that he is both highly intelligent and very well read in European history and the history of modern ideas," Bawer wrote. "There is reason to be deeply concerned about all these things, and to want to see them addressed forcefully by government leaders." Breivik had "a legitimate concern about genuine problems," Bawer continued, even if his solution was "unspeakably evil."

In the months after the attacks, Bawer hardened his position further. In 2012, he published a short e-book that sharply denounced the response to the attacks from the "left-wing cultural elite" and the international media, whom he described as "apologists for radical Islam." The book, tellingly, is titled *The New Quislings*, after the Norwegian Nazi collaborationist leader Vidkun Quisling. In it, Bawer suggests explicitly that people who tolerate immigration from Muslim-majority regions are analogous to those who allowed Hitler to take over their countries. The government and the media are, in Bawer's argument, class A and class B traitors.

The Mother of Eurabia

When you try to find out what might have caused otherwise reasonable people such as Bawer to become foaming Muslim-tide extremists, you keep running into the same little old woman. She is the grandmotherly inspiration of authors and activists, the inventor of the word "Eurabia," the coiner of the popular angry bloggers' insult "dhimmitude," and the widely acknowledged matriarch of the movement. Almost every Muslim-tide book written since September 11 has drawn on the writings of Gisèle Littman, a self-educated, Egyptian-born, Swiss-English writer who publishes under the pen name Bat Ye'or (Hebrew for "daughter of the Nile").

The most famous Bat Ye'or book—the one whose title put a new portmanteau word into the language and effectively catalyzed an entire movement—is *Eurabia: The Euro-Arab Axis*, published in 2005, and a surprise hit in the years after the September 11 attacks. It has been lauded by conservative popular historians such as Niall Ferguson (who called it "prophetic") and Sir Martin Gilbert (who said it helped prove that "the European idea is being subverted by Islamic hostility to the very ethics and values of Europe itself").[3] As a result, you might assume that this book makes a credible case for Islamic ambitions in Europe. Instead, her book's purported dark heart is not anything Islamic or Arabic but rather an obscure Brussels committee called the Euro-Arab Dialogue.

In the real world, the Euro-Arab Dialogue was a diplomatic talking shop created in 1973 by the European Economic Community, the precursor to the European Union, to improve diplomatic relations with the Arab states in the wake of the OPEC oil crisis and the Yom Kippur War. Its original goals of helping the cause of Middle East peace and improving trade relations across the Mediterranean went nowhere, in large part because the Europeans wanted it to be an economic forum and the Arabs wanted it to be political.[4] In 1979, after only four meetings, the Dialogue was suspended. Attempts to relaunch it in 1990 and 2008 were widely regarded as failures. It has never had any policy power and wields no political influence. In fact, it is so universally regarded as an irrelevance that it was over-shadowed by two later efforts to improve relations between Europe and its Middle Eastern and North African neighbours, the EU's 1995 Barcelona Process and French president Nicolas Sarkozy's 2008 Union for the Mediterranean.*

In the mind of Gisèle Littman, though, this sleepy committee and its successors are orchestrating a continent-wide Islamic take-over. The Euro-Arab Dialogue, she writes in *Eurabia*, "has been in the vanguard of engineering a convergence between Europe and the Islamic states of North Africa and the Middle East . . . a new entity—with political, economic, religious, cultural and media components—superimposed on Europe by powerful governmental lobbies. . . . What is emerging is a new Eurabian culture with its own dogma, preachers, axioms and rules." This political dialogue, she argues, is one of "the main steps of a transformation that has

---

* Far from being the vanguard of an anti-Western takeover, these initiatives were lauded by Israel, denounced by Colonel Muammar Gaddafi as a foil for European imperialism, and rejected by the Turks as a ploy to keep them out of EU membership.

already begun in Europe, the birth of a new *dhimmi* civilization: Eurabia." To support this claim, she offers only a thin soup of assertions that bracket passages from anodyne committee reports. That was all it took to earn her great credibility among a generation of writers, activists and politicians.

Littman had built her reputation on her earlier Bat Ye'or books, a series of amateur histories of the Middle East that offered harsh portraits of the repressions and humiliations suffered by Christians and Jews under Islamic regimes, from the seventh through the late twentieth century. Littman's family were Egyptian Jews who fled to Europe in the 1950s, an experience that must have inspired her to adapt *dhimmi*, a neutral Arabic term for religious minorities whose presence was tolerated (sometimes roughly) in Islamic states, into dhimmitude, her darkly menacing word for "subjected, non-Muslim individuals or people [who] accept the restrictive and humiliating subordination to an ascendant Islamic power to avoid enslavement or death"—or, in practice, anyone who tolerates Muslim immigrants or recognizes their religion. It has become a word used endlessly by anti-Muslim bloggers and their fans to dismiss critics or liberals as Eurabian sellouts. However popular it is online, the concept has no credibility. Even the Middle East historian Bernard Lewis, who has been strongly critical of contemporary Islam, dismissed dhimmitude as a historical myth, comparable to the mirror-image Islamic myth of a "golden age" of multifaith harmony. "Like many myths," he wrote, "both contain significant elements of truth, and the historic truth is in its usual place, somewhere in the middle between the extremes."[5]

Littman, however, is not a historian but a radical activist. This was starkly apparent from the mid-1990s, when she gained her first taste of public renown by employing her dhimmitude arguments to bolster the Serbian cause in Bosnia. In a series of interviews and speeches, she popularized the idea that Bosnia's Muslim-plurality population, at that point being attacked by Serb militias, were the war's real threat, and their attackers were actually "Serbian resistance movements" against "the gradual Muslim penetration of Europe."[6] In 1995, she delivered a speech at the Lord Byron Foundation for Balkan Studies, a group dominated by Srdja Trifkovic, the adviser to and spokesman for Radovan Karadzic, the Bosnian Serb warlord who, only months before the talk, had organized the Srebrenica massacre. Littman's speech championed the arguments made by the Serbian radicals: that the Muslims of Bosnia and Kosovo have a centuries-old plot to take over Europe, and that, as she said, "suddenly the recent crisis in Yugoslavia offered a new chance for [the plot's] reincarnation in a multi-religious Muslim Bosnian state. What a chance! A Muslim state again in the heartland of Europe. And we know the rest, the sufferings, the miseries, the trials of the war."

This unsavoury background has not prevented scores of writers and journalists from believing in Littman's shadowy plot. Shortly after the publication of *Eurabia*, Oriana Fallaci, in the final episode of her journalistic career, eagerly adopted and amplified the Bat Ye'or argument. "Europe is no longer Europe, it is 'Eurabia,' a colony of Islam, where the Islamic invasion does not proceed only in a physical sense, but also in a mental and cultural sense," Fallaci told the *Wall Street Journal* in 2005. Mind you, she had already embraced the demographic claims behind the Muslim-tide argument in the least subtle fashion, writing, in her 2002 Italian bestseller *The Rage and the Pride* that the "sons of Allah . . . they multiply like rats."

Language like this seemed to find a new licence after the September 11 attacks. Amid the public anxiety and distrust of those years, it was hard for many people to make the distinction between Islamic terrorism and ordinary Muslims. And here, fully prepared for such an event, was a voice declaring loudly that such a distinction had never existed. The most immediate effect of Littman's oeuvre was to inspire a set of extremist blogs dotted with her neologisms: Gates of Vienna, founded by the American activist Ned May, which warns of a "worldwide jihad," calls for the expulsion of all Muslims from Europe and had a close relationship with Breivik's friends and enablers; Atlas Shrugs, run by the American anti-Muslim firebrand Pamela Gellar (author of books such as *Stop the Islamization of America: A Practical Guide to the Resistance*); and Jihad Watch, run by the provocateur Robert Spencer, author of such memorable titles as *The Truth about Muhammad: Founder of the World's Most Intolerant Religion*.

Such shrill messages, joined in the angry years of the Iraq War by established American anti-immigration and anti-Muslim voices such as Daniel Pipes and Patrick Buchanan, slowly rose from the extremist fringe of the Internet into more respectable circles, and eventually came to play a powerful role in the post-Bush Tea Party branch of the Republican Party. Along the way, they linked up with an older, more potent set of fears.

The Self-Hating Westerners

"Can you have the same Europe with different people?"

Those nine words, penned by the *Financial Times* columnist Christopher Caldwell and printed across the cover of many editions of his 2009 book, *Reflections on the Revolution in Europe: Immigration, Islam, and the West,* are a succinct summary of the anxiety driving the Muslim-tide movement, as well as a key demonstration of the essential illogic of its arguments. After all, as we shall see in the next chapter, recent Muslim immigrants are no more "different" than the earlier, larger waves of religious minorities who contribute to the current populations of most Western countries. Still, this has become a widely held public opinion about Muslim immigrants: they are different, and they will force *us* to be different.

His argument is novel in that it does not simply claim that Muslims are plotting to take over the West. Instead, he blames the victim: the West, he says, has morally and spiritually collapsed into wide-open vulnerability. "The spiritual tawdriness Islamic immigrants perceive in the modern West is not imaginary," Caldwell begins. "It may be Europe's biggest liability in preserving its culture." Like those earlier Muslim-tide authors, he also sees Muslims as disloyal arrivals whose birth rates will swamp the West and whose faith is better described as an ideology. "Imagine that the West, at the height of the Cold War, had received a mass inflow of immigrants from Communist countries who were ambivalent about which side they supported. . . . Something similar is taking place now." But to this he adds something new: admiration, even envy, for the spiritual strength and organizational coherence of Muslims and a corresponding horror at the disappearance of such qualities in the West. His book, like many others of recent years, gains its potency by resurrecting two powerful, long-dormant concepts.

The first is the clash of civilizations. When Samuel Huntington gave that old phrase a new lease on life shortly after the end of the Cold War with his book *The Clash of Civilizations and the Remaking of World Order*, his argument sounded, to more reasonable ears, like a modern resurrection of the medieval vision of competing religious empires—a scenario that had been eclipsed by centuries of cultural convergence and economic interconnection. But after September 11, the notion of monolithic, incompatible "civilizations" suddenly appealed to Islamic extremists in the East as much as to the Muslim-tide authors and politicians in the West. Among both Islamic radicals and anti-Islamic radicals, it became popular once again to speak of a spiritual no man's land between two distinct blocs of humanity.

The second seductive concept is the decline of the West. Even before Oswald Spengler's 1918 bestseller of that title, it had been popular, during moments of economic or military difficulty, for some conservatives to claim that the societies of the West had brought it upon themselves with their "moral decline"—usually a reference to the diminished power of the Church after the Enlightenment.

This combination of ideas—*civilizations* and *decline*—gave the Muslim-tide argument a powerful new kick of self-blame for Europeans (and, for some Americans, a potent sense of being threatened not just by Islamic beliefs but also by weak-kneed European secularism). "It is certain that Europe will emerge changed from its confrontation with Islam," concludes Caldwell, who sees both the Enlightenment and the liberation movements of the 1960s as terrible mistakes that caused a collapse of European Christianity into postmodern decadence. "When an insecure, malleable, relativistic culture meets a culture that is anchored, confident, and strengthened by common doctrines, it is generally the former that changes to suit the latter."

Caldwell offered the polite version of this argument. But there were writers willing to express it more bluntly. One of the most successful British books of this century's first decade was *Londonistan,* by the *Daily Mail* columnist Melanie Phillips, which began with the quite plausible argument that London had become a hotbed of Islamic-terrorist organizing (certainly true at the decade's outset), and then went on to claim that the majority of British Muslims are believers in jihad and sharia. Britain has become "hollowed out," she wrote, by "the onslaught mounted by secular nihilists against the country's Judeo-Christian values . . . a debauched and disorderly culture of instant gratification, with disintegrating families, feral children and violence, squalor and vulgarity on the streets." To Phillips's mind, it was our secular amorality that had brought about Islamic radicalism.

If Caldwell is the cool-headed preacher of original sin and pending end times, his comic-opera choirmaster is the Canadian Mark Steyn. After spending decades as a well-regarded writer on musical theatre, publishing such books as *Broadway Babies Say Goodnight*, Steyn, like Bruce Bawer, took a sharp turn after September 11 into the more corrosive (and lucrative) territory of sarcasm-laced political commentary. In the *Wall Street Journal*, in Canada's *Maclean's*, and in his blog and breezy books, he won headlines by popularizing the claims of the Bat Ye'or books ("Islam itself is a political project") and adding a supercharged take on the demographic claim. "By some projections, the EU's population will be 40 per cent Muslim by 2025," he argued in one article; in several others, that the continent would be Muslim-majority by century's end; and in another, that "Europe will be semi-Islamic in its politico-cultural character within a generation" or that every European "under the age of 40— make that 60, if not 75—is all but guaranteed to end his days living in an Islamified Europe."

Modernity has feminized the West and rendered it meek, Steyn argues repeatedly, and that feminization has led it to abort itself into nonexistence. Muslims, he writes, are destined to take over the Western world because "they've calculated that our entire civilization lacks the will to see them off." Steyn's works appealed to Anders Breivik, whose manifesto quoted them several times. And indeed, while Steyn is far from being a violent or militaristic figure, he ends his bestseller *America Alone: The End of the World as We Know It* with a passage that seems to have prefigured the Norwegian's apocalyptic rhetoric: "We have been shirking too long, and that's unworthy of a great civilization. To see off the new Dark Ages will be tough and demanding. The alternative will be worse."

Millions of otherwise moderate and reasonable people have bought these books, enjoyed them, and sometimes praised and repeated their arguments. Most readers, I suspect, are not subscribing to these authors' more ornate conspiracies or darker claims of pending catastrophe. Rather, they are seeking a narrative that might help explain the bewildering appearance of visibly different Muslim communities in their cities, and the near-simultaneous eruptions of Islamist violence that marked the first years of this century. Much as a rumbling distrust of Catholics and Jews among earlier generations was supported by a string of hyperbolic books making similar claims, these Muslim-tide works provide most readers with more of a reassurance than a call to arms. A small minority of readers, however, have been inspired to support a new type of politics.

III THE PARTIES OF EURABIA

WHEN I VISITED Geert Wilders in The Hague two years before the Norwegian murders, what surprised me was not his louche English or his famous bottle-blond coif, but his taste in art. The paintings he chose to adorn his parliamentary office suite were not what you'd expect from the leader of the radically anti-Muslim Party For Freedom (PVV): not the heroic horsebound realism of an archconservative revanchist, nor the stark abstractions of a free-market libertarian. No, this was hippie art, the sort of rock-poster phantasmagoria popular among velvet revolutionaries, with pert-breasted naked girls transmogrifying into pianos and rainbow-hued evocations of cosmic love. And in these psychedelic artifacts you could spot the secret to his success: Wilders did not become the third most powerful politician in the Netherlands on a platform of intolerance, but rather on a platform of claiming not to tolerate those who are intolerant of the Dutch lifestyle. All of whom just happen to be Muslim.

"Whatever colour or sexual preference, whatever people have, it doesn't matter as they're all welcome in our party and we don't discriminate in any way," he told me. His party won 15% of the votes in the 2010 national election with a message that included the deportation of Muslims and the outlawing of the Koran. It was the first of several anti-Muslim parties swept into substantial election victories across northern and western Europe at the height of the economic crisis.

A party opposed to religious extremism sounds, frankly, like a perfectly reasonable idea, I told him. Would he expand his message to include problems of Christian zealotry? Wilders bristled at this suggestion and told me there could be no comparison. "I see many differences between Islam and other religions," he said. "In fact, I see Islam not so much as a religion as much as an ideology. As I see it, the aim of the Islamic ideology is to dominate and to submit the Western societies to their belief, and this is unlike the other religions. I say that Islam is not another branch on the tree of religions—it has to be put in the corner of totalitarian ideologies. That's why I compare it with communism and fascism—I see the comparisons between the Koran and *Mein Kampf*."[7]

Wilders then gave me a lecture about what he calls "al-Hijra, the Islamic doctrine of migration," in which Muslim believers follow Koranic commands ordering them to migrate to foreign lands and have great numbers of children, acting as Trojan Horses bent on civilizational domination. This is a popular concept on the fringes of the Eurabia movement. It has escaped wider notice in large part because it has not a word of support in the text of the Koran and has never been advocated, in speech or in print, by any Muslim leader, however radical—with the sole exception of the late Libyan dictator Muammar Gaddafi, who once gave a speech calling on Muslims to take over Europe through migration. (Gaddafi, far from being an Islamic figurehead, was mainly known for his imprisonment and mass murder of Islamists, and also for forbidding his people's migration.)

Such gaps in logic had not stopped Wilders from becoming a very successful politician. "I believe that we will be able to redefine the meaning of what is mainstream in this country," he told me. And to a certain extent he has already succeeded—not just in his own country.

The first decade of this century saw an explosion of Eurabia parties. In neighbouring Denmark, the Danish People's Party—whose platform often sounds like parts of Breivik's manifesto—became the third-largest force in parliament, with 14% of the vote. In Finland, the even more harshly xenophobic True Finns won a fifth of the vote. The Sweden Democrats, whose platform is almost entirely anti-Muslim, won their first parliamentary seats, 20 out of 349, in the 2010 election. And in Norway, despite the outpouring of national outrage following Breivik's attack, views similar to his had already entered mainstream politics. In 2010, Christian Tybring-Gjedde, the finance critic for the opposition Progress Party and head of its Oslo branch, wrote a furious attack on immigration in which he described Muslim immigrants as having "the goal of stabbing our culture in the back" and warned that their presence "will tear our country apart." And this was *after* the party had purged its radical anti-immigrant faction.

The Norwegian massacre did nothing to dim the popularity of these views. A week after Breivik's slayings, I dropped in on Arne Tumyr, an Oslo right-wing activist and former newspaper editor whose group SIAN (Stop Islamization of Norway) included Breivik among its supporters. He told me he welcomed the attention the attacks brought to his cause. "Of course we have nothing to do with his violence—we have sent him into the dark," he quickly added. "But this new debate is a great opportunity for us to educate Norwegians about the truth, which is that Muslims are not a religion, they are a political fifth column out to take over our part of the world."

The Angry Banker

None of these political precedents prepared anyone for the strange and outsized phenomenon of Thilo Sarrazin. A most unlikely figure, this German central banker was a senior figure in the centre-left Social Democratic Party, and a man who seemed almost a caricature of straitlaced Berlin moderation. This contrast, rather than the book's arguments, may have been why his *Germany Abolishes Itself: How We Are Putting Our Country at Risk* became the most popular political book of postreunification Germany, selling 1.2 million copies in little more than three months in 2010. But the upshot was that a man of the respectable left had effectively resurrected a set of ideas about religious minorities that had been banished from German thought for six decades.

His bestseller began with the tropes of the Eurabia literature, complete with its decline-of-the-West anomie. "Demographically, the enormous fertility of Muslim migrants is a threat to the cultural and civilizational equilibrium of an ageing Europe," Sarrazin wrote. "I don't want the country of my grandchildren and great-grandchildren to become largely Muslim, to have Turkish and Arabic spoken over wide areas, to have women wearing headscarves and the daily rhythm of life dictated by the call of the muezzin." In interviews, he expanded on the idea, indicting four million Turko-Germans in a conspiracy: "The Turks are conquering Germany as the Kosovars have conquered Kosovo: by a higher birth rate." Germany's Turks, of course, did not invade the country but were invited to come, beginning in the late 1950s, in order to fill huge labour shortages in low-skilled fields. And then, after being asked to stay and settle, they were denied citizenship for the better part of forty years, until citizenship laws were reformed in 1999. For this reason, Turks, who in other countries have integrated well into the economy and the educational system and slipped easily into citizenship, have had difficulty in Germany.[8] They also, as we shall see, do not have particularly high birth rates.

What made Sarrazin's work stand out from the shelfload of similar works, however, was the way he laced it with racial-superiority theories. While he did not quite say that Muslims are genetically inferior, he argued at some length that Jews (whom he treats as a race rather than as a multiracial religion or culture) are genetically superior to German Christians; their apparently higher IQ levels are not a result of education or culture but, he says, partly of genetics. Readers are left to imagine where Muslims are supposed to stand on this step-ladder of spiritual intelligence, but his language left little doubt. His chapter on demography is subtitled "More Children of the Clever, Before It Is Too Late," and his most famous passage declares that Germans, by allowing Turks into their community, "have accepted as inevitable that Germany will be smaller and dumber."

What impact did Sarrazin's book have on German politics? That's a more ambiguous question. "Rarely has a man influenced the German public discourse as much as Sarrazin has done with his book," the newsweekly *Der Spiegel* wrote. But the nature of that influence is uncertain. He was fired from the board of the Deutsche Bundesbank, though not from the Social Democrats. Chancellor Angela Merkel used the book's popularity to make some vague statements about Islam and immigration, and famously to denounce multiculturalism (which has never been practised or advocated in Germany). And both major parties finally acknowledged that Germany has left millions of immigrants and their offspring trapped in a non-citizen nether-world, and that the country needs to invest in proper immigrant-integration programmes and citizenship initiatives for the next waves of immigrants. In that sense, the book may have been beneficial to Germany. But Sarrazin, by dint of his book's popularity and his mainstream respectability, also helped embed a set of false notions in the public imagination. Although *Germany Abolishes Itself* faced con-siderable criticism for its tone and stance, the media made few efforts to correct its false claims about Muslim immigrants, their population growth and their degree of integration.

And just as the book's popularity was peaking, a very similar con-troversy was erupting on the other side of the Atlantic.

IV A VERY AMERICAN INVASION

THERE WAS NOTHING ABOUT the Aoude family that ought to have attracted the nation's attention. Nawal Aoude, 25, works as a respiratory technician, and she and her husband, Nader, a 35-year-old government worker, fill their days in Dearborn, Michigan, with the usual rhythms and habits of American suburbia: football, jogging, amateur theatre, religion, family, mortgage payments, work. The most threatening event in their lives was the somewhat difficult birth of their son Naseem, in August 2011.

Nader's dad had immigrated from Lebanon decades earlier and worked in the Detroit auto industry without experiencing any significant discrimination. Nader and Nawal, fully integrated Americans, had no reason to expect they would encounter any, either. But at the end of 2011 they found themselves the target of an organized national attack. The couple had allowed a television-producer friend to bring cameras into their house earlier that year for a TLC documentary series, *All-American Muslim*, which followed the routine domestic travails of several Arab-American families in Dearborn. One episode chronicled the birth of Naseem and its attendant anxieties.

An evangelical group, the Florida Family Association, launched the attack against the show, calling for a boycott and denouncing it as part of an Islamist plot. "*All-American Muslim* is propaganda clearly designed to counter legitimate and present-day concerns about many Muslims who are advocating Islamic fundamentalism and Sharia law," declared David Caton, the reformed porn addict and evangelical crusader who runs the Family Association. "The show profiles only Muslims that appear to be ordinary folks while excluding many Islamic believers whose agenda poses a clear and present danger to the liberties and traditional values that the majority of Americans cherish."

His association called for an advertiser boycott, the sort of thing that, given his group's obscure profile, would usually be ignored. This time, something struck a chord. Two of the show's main advertisers—the home-improvement chain Lowe's and the online travel retailer Kayak.com—withdrew their sponsorship. By itself, this could have been dismissed as one of those periodic eruptions of Florida culture-war extremism that are an established part of the political tectonics of the United States. But it occurred at exactly the moment when the same arguments about Muslims entered national politics and became a feature of the 2012 presidential campaign.

Newt Gingrich led the way with a 2010 speech, recounted on the front page of the *New York Times* the week of the All-American Muslim boycott, in which he'd warned of the dangers of "stealth jihad"—a concept invented by Robert Spencer, the Jihad Watch blogger and anti-Muslim activist. "I believe Sharia is a mortal threat to the survival of freedom in the United States and in the world as we know it," Gingrich told the American Enterprise Institute. He suggested that this is a relevant issue in the United States, whose Constitution prohibits any religious role in law, because ordinary Muslims are secretly carrying out a plot. "I think it's that straightforward and that real. . . . Stealth jihadis use political, cultural, societal, religious, intellectual tools; violent jihadis use violence. But in fact they're both engaged in jihad, and they're both seeking to impose the same end state, which is to replace Western civilization with a radical imposition of Sharia." This argument was adopted by other candidates, like Rick Santorum (who called the stealth imposition of Islamic law a "new existential threat to America"). Candidates who didn't embrace it, like Mitt Romney, received harsh criticism from the Tea Party branch of the Republicans.

Where did this language come from? Islamic terrorism and extremism had been part of American political debate for a decade, but this was something new. In the years leading up to 2010, it had gradually become acceptable, in some establishment political and media circles, to assert that ordinary Muslims are the problem, that Islamic immigrants and their offspring may be disloyal, and that the religion and its followers should not be tolerated in the same way others are. Such ideas—which as we will see in chapter 3 are nearly identical to those once expressed in the United States about Roman Catholic and Jewish immigrants—stayed far outside the mainstream during the George W. Bush presidency. But two things happened after 2008: the Republican Party experienced a post-Bush power vacuum, which gave new candidates from the anti-Muslim right far more latitude, and the Muslim-tide writers and activists joined forces and attracted major funding and media attention.

In many ways, they had become an organized lobby. An investigation conducted in 2011 by the Center for American Progress found that between 2001 and 2009, Robert Spencer, Pamela Gellar of Atlas Shrugs and three other formerly fringe anti-Muslim bloggers and activists had together managed to attract $42.6 million in funding from seven mainstream conservative foundations, none of which had previously backed such voices. That money bought them an outsized lobbying and media presence. They spent almost $17 million to send 28 million swing-state voters copies of the DVD *Obsession: Radical Islam's War against the West*, a film whose content is largely identical to Breivik's manifesto and features commentary by Bat Ye'or and similar figures. The new movement attracted mainstream media attention during the 2010 furor over the "ground zero mosque," a proposed Islamic cultural and religious centre in lower Manhattan. That outrage was largely the work of Spencer and Gellar, but it soon won the sympathy of at least four Republican leadership candidates.[9]

By the time the U.S. election season was fully underway in 2012, there had been a subtle but significant shift in the language and rhetoric of public debates. Before, it had been quite acceptable for American politicians to identify and denounce Islamic fundamentalism and radicalism, and even for conservatives to accuse mainstream organizations and leaders of being agents or enablers of extreme Islam. But ordinary Muslim Americans were not targeted, since it was widely understood, even by much of the Christian right, that immigrants from Muslim-majority countries and their descendants were generally well-integrated Americans with moderate views. But something changed in the years after Barack Obama's 2008 election. It was partly attributable to the 2009 shooting rampage at Fort Hood, Texas, and the intercepted 2010 Times Square bomb plot, which together created a sense of growing homegrown extremism (they proved to be only coincidental: there was no increase in extremism or terrorism-related arrests in the years afterwards). But the lobbying and media attention generated by the Muslim-tide authors, activists and politicians played a large part.

This shift in emphasis seemed to penetrate not only the conservative media and Republican politics but also, to a surprising degree, official and bureaucratic thought. In 2011, Americans learned that the FBI had been giving its agents a counterterrorism course that described many ordinary Islamic believers as part of an "insurgency" whose threat is not so much "radical" as "a normal assertion of orthodox ideology," and whose stealth techniques include "immigration" and "lawsuits." In theory, any American Muslim immigrant should be investigated, as should any Muslim who, in response, sues the Bureau for harassment. One of the books the course recommended to agents was Robert Spencer's *The Truth about Muhammad*, one of Anders Breivik's influences.

This alarmed veteran counterterrorism officers, whose work has relied on building relations of trust with American Muslim communities.[10] But their complaints were ignored. In significant sections of US policing, the entire Muslim community had become a target. In 2012 the New York Police Department admitted that it was keeping surveillance files on thousands of "second- and third-generation Americans specifically because they were Muslims," in the words of an Associated Press investigation, even though they were not suspected of anything. Rather than condemning or ending the practice, Mayor Michael Bloomberg defended it with words that seemed to summarize the new attitude: "We're doing the right thing."

It had become politically acceptable, and possibly even politically beneficial, to admit to targeting an entire ethnic group for surveillance. For a substantial number of voters had come to believe the myth. One poll in August, 2010 found that 31% of Americans, and 52% of Republicans, agreed that President Barack Obama "sympathizes with the goals of Islamic fundamentalists who want to impose Islamic law around the world."[11]

The real danger here is that Americans, who have avoided the politics of racial division for more than a generation, will start to become exactly what their enemies accuse them of being. Islamic extremists, including Osama bin Laden, have always argued that the world is divided into two irreconcilable civilizations, and that their violent cause is justified because the West is waging war against all Muslims. Western leaders have so far generally been careful, even at the height of the Iraq and Afghanistan wars, to counter this perception by embracing and protecting the Muslim communities within their populations. Today, however, the extremist argument is in danger of becoming real, as the Muslim-tide movement's ideas infiltrate the hierarchies of politics, media and security. Many of the Eurabia activists, as we have seen, are in agreement with the radical Islamist view of the world. Anders Breivik devoted long passages of his manifesto to his unabashed admiration for bin Laden's philosophy and tactics, and writers like Melanie Phillips and Christopher Caldwell are readily willing to express admiration for what they see as the religious strength of an insurgent Muslim civilization.

This formerly fringe movement has captured too much ground by stealth, using little more than emotional appeals to fear. Before we let that fear overtake our political principles and rupture our social harmony, we ought to stop and pay close attention to the well-documented facts about this latest wave of immigration. We know from tragic historical precedent that a few dark suspicions about a new group of neighbours, combined with a collection of false and misleading facts, can do enormous, irreversible damage to a society. It is time to put our fears aside, and let the facts prevail.

TWO
THE
FACTS

WHO ARE THESE PEOPLE? It's a reasonable question to ask when new neighbours move into town. We want to know if they resemble us, how many of them there are, what customs they're bringing from their old home, how much they are likely to change and whether they pose a threat. In the case of Muslim immigrants, there are now hundreds of books and videos that purport to offer answers to these questions. Unfortunately, the answers they provide are angry, alarmist, and based on little more than the xenophobic predilections of their authors, backed with statistics and claims hand-picked to bolster their argument of presumed menace. Genuinely curious readers are left to choose between the screeching volumes of the Muslim-tide genre and a competing raft of books, just as selective and one-sided in their approach, intended to defend Islam as a religion of peace. For the genuinely curious reader, there is pitifully little impartial information.

I am taking a different approach. In this chapter, I examine in good faith each of the major factual claims of the Muslim-tide movement, using the most comprehensive and up-to-date research, scholarship, statistics and surveys my researchers and I were able to find. I have divided the claims into three major areas: those related to the population growth of Muslims and whether they will reach majority status in any Western country; those that question whether Muslims are becoming integrated members of their new countries or are remaining segregated into "parallel societies"; and those that look into the radical, extremist, violent or angry views and ambitions held by Muslims in the West.

I present all the facts relevant to each claim, even when those facts happen to support the claim. My purpose here is not to defend a religion or its practitioners, but to find a way to distinguish the genuine threats and worries that should concern us—and there are several—from those that are baseless. Rather than seeking simply to "debunk" myths and false assumptions by searching for facts that happen to support my hypothesis, I have taken great care to also highlight the genuinely alarming facts. While I conclude that the Muslim-tide hypothesis on the whole has no merit, that does not mean that it is based entirely on untruths. What I am offering here, I hope, is an opportunity to think clearly and dispassionately about a very heated subject.

I POPULATION

THE CENTRAL IMAGE in all of the Muslim-tide literature is that of a population being swamped by strangers. The theory holds that the numbers of Islamic immigrants and their offspring are growing so quickly that Muslims will become a majority in the West in coming decades. Once they're a majority, they will overwhelm the fast-shrinking host population with their beliefs and religious laws. This theory relies on a few common-sense assumptions. New immigrants have big families. Muslim countries are often overpopulated, and have been known to experience rapid population growth. Westerners have very small families, on average, and many Western countries have shrinking populations. The proportion of Muslims in the West has increased.

As a result reasonable people might conclude that Muslims are going to become a majority, or at least a very large plurality, in Western countries. Even if you don't buy the civilizational-takeover claims of the Eurabia books, you would have good reason to believe their basic demographic case. The trouble is that it's based on some fundamental misunderstandings, well understood by scholars but generally absent from the public debate. In making this basic demographic argument—that there is, in fact, a tide of Muslims—the Muslim-tide movement has strayed furthest from the truth.

CLAIM:

The Muslim population in the West is growing fast and will soon become a majority in Europe.

Europe will have a Muslim majority by the end of the twenty-first century at the very latest. **- Bernard Lewis**

The European Union will be well on its way to majority Muslim by 2035. As things stand, Muslims are already the primary source of population growth in English cities. Can a society become increasingly Islamic in its demographic profile without becoming increasingly Islamic in its political character? **- Mark Steyn**

BECAUSE WE SEE a lot of veiled women in our big cities these days, and because those women usually have a lot of children, we Westerners fear that Muslims will become a majority. Several prominent writers have suggested that Muslims will become the largest religious group in Europe by 2050, or by the end of the twenty-first century; others have hypothesized Muslim majorities within decades in individual European countries or US states.

Such things have been known to occur. Faster-breeding immigrants have overtaken host communities in New England, for example, where Roman Catholics became a majority in the twentieth century, displacing the Protestant majority that had existed since the Puritan settlements. Catholics also became the largest group in the Netherlands in the twentieth century because of higher birth rates. And Muslims displaced Orthodox Christians as the majority in

Kosovo in the late eighteenth and early nineteenth centuries due to higher birth rates and gradual in-migration.

Is that happening throughout the West today? The superficial evidence makes it look that way, since the Muslim population in Europe has grown very fast. In 1950, there were probably fewer than 300,000 Muslims in the 27 countries that now make up the European Union. Today there are somewhere between 15 and 20 million—between 3% and 4% of the continent's 500 million people. Some Muslim groups have very high birth rates: Bangladeshis in Britain, to choose one of the more extreme examples, have on average 3 children per family, while "White British" have only 1.7.[1] So while only 4% of Britons are Muslim, at that rate their proportion could double in 20 years. If a country's fertility rate falls below 2.1 children per family, its population will stop growing.* At the moment, non-Muslim Europeans have very low fertility rates, averaging 1.5 children per family across the continent; by 2030, the population will begin shrinking. But Muslims in Europe average 2.2 per family across the continent,[2] which means their communities are growing—and they continue to immigrate, adding more young, highly fertile people to the mix.

On the face of it, it seems plausible that Muslim population growth could be exponential, and that Muslims could be headed toward majority status. How soon would this happen? Until recently, nobody really knew, since there were no reliable data on the size and growth of Muslim-immigrant populations. People speculated and guessed,

---

* The total fertility rate (TFR) is a calculation, based on birth statistics, of the total number of children an average woman will have in her life—in other words, the average family size. A TFR of 2.1 is needed to keep a country's population stable. Above 2.1, the population grows; at 2.0 or less, it will eventually shrink. All this chapter's national TFR figures are taken from *World Population Prospects: The 2010 Revision,* published by the Population Division of the United Nations Department of Economic and Social Affairs and found at www.un.org/esa/population.

and the Eurabia authors seized on these guesses and amplified them.

The last few years, however, have seen a revolution in the statistical understanding of Muslim immigrants in Europe and North America. Recently, neutral academic or government institutions have produced several large-scale projections of Muslim populations, based on reliable statistics.

The largest and most comprehensive of these projections was conducted in 2011 by the Washington-based Pew Research Center.[3] Dozens of scholars drew on the most recent and accurate statistical and demographic information to produce a detailed look at the future of the global Muslim population. The study examines the "Europe" conventionally used in the Muslim-tide literature: the major European Union states plus Switzerland and Norway, a territory encompassing 405 million people and the countries with the highest Muslim immigration rates.* Its Muslim population in 2010 was 18.2 million, or 4.5% of the population. The study finds that if current immigration levels and birth rate trends are extrapolated, Europe's Muslim population will expand to 29.8 million, or 7.1% of the population, by 2030. The study also examines the widest possible definition of "Europe," one that includes all 50 European states and territories including Russia, whose long-established population of 16.3 million Muslims almost doubles the continent's total, as well as historically Muslim countries such as Albania and Bosnia. By this measure, the Muslim population of this wider Europe in 2010 was 44.1 million, or 6% of the population, and it will expand to 58 million, or 8% of the wider continent's population, by 2030, largely because of very low non-Muslim fertility rates in Russia.

---

* This includes Austria, Belgium, Denmark, Finland, France, Germany, Greece, Ireland, Italy, Luxembourg, the Netherlands, Norway, Portugal, Spain, Sweden, Switzerland and the United Kingdom—the 17 countries with the largest populations and the highest Muslim immigration rates.

This trend will vary by country: France's Muslims, the largest group in Western Europe, will increase from 4.7 million to 6.9 million (or 10.3% of the population) by 2030; Germany will see a far more modest increase, from 4.1 million to 5.5 million (7.1%); and the Muslim population of the United Kingdom will nearly double from 2.9 million (4.6%) in 2010 to 5.6 million (8.2%) in 2030. At this rate, it's just barely possible that Muslims could represent more than 9.5% of the European population (including Russia) by 2050, a point that would likely represent a peak—if immigration from Islamic countries remains fairly high, if non-Muslim fertility remains very low, and if integration continues to be a slow and difficult process for Muslims. But none of these factors are certain at all. It is equally likely that the Muslim population will level off somewhere around the 8% mark.

This is not exactly exponential growth. In the 20 years between 1990 and 2010, Europe added 14.5 million Muslims to its population; in the 20 years between 2010 and 2030, it will add 14 million more to a larger base population. In other words, the rate of Muslim population growth is slowing. By 2030, the Pew analysts conclude, Europe's Muslims will be reproducing at the rate of 2.0 children per family while non-Muslim fertility will have increased slightly to 1.6 children (there has been a slow but steady rise in non-Muslim fertility in recent years). There are no signs of Muslims becoming a European majority, or even a very large minority.

North America has far fewer Muslims, but they are a very new, young group—63% of all American Muslims are first-generation immigrants, and 71% of those immigrants arrived after 1990[4]—and as a result of this infusion the population is growing faster. In the United States, Muslims will more than double over the next 20 years, from 2.6 million in 2010 to 6.2 million in 2030, making them, at 1.7% of the population, almost as numerous as Jews and Episcopalians.

American Muslims have an average of 2.5 children, compared with 2.1 for all Americans. In Canada, the Muslim population will nearly triple over the same period, from 940,000 to 2.7 million, rising from 2.8% to 6.6% of the Canadian population. Their fertility, of 2.4 per family, is higher than the average Canadian fertility of 1.7, though it too is dropping. This is in large part because Canada's current Muslim immigrants are more likely to come from countries such as Pakistan, whose population is largely rural and more fertile.

The Pew findings on Europe are supported by other recent statistical projections. One was conducted in 2010 by British demographer Eric Kaufmann and a team at the International Institute for Applied Systems Analysis in Austria. It came to similar conclusions, projecting that the Muslim population in the European Union could reach 10% by 2050. A few low-fertility countries such as Sweden and Austria could see 15% Muslim populations by mid-century if their immigration levels do not change.[5]

So did a 2011 study by the US Congressional Research Service.[6] It projects that by 2030 the 27 countries of the EU, plus non-members Norway and Switzerland, could together have 30 million Muslims, representing 7% of the population.

None of these studies project anything close to a Muslim majority. And even the highest estimate of these trends would not produce a Muslim majority in any Western country during the twenty-first century. Islam would become the second-place religion in one or two more countries (it already has that status in France), and reach third place in a few others, but only if we assume that the children of religious Muslims are themselves religious Muslims, and that the next immigrant waves from other regions won't drive their proportions down.

What about the more distant future? If we assume that the higher Muslim birth rates continue indefinitely, you might think that

Muslims could become a European majority at some point, perhaps before the end of the twenty-second century. To believe that, you need to believe two other things: that Muslims inevitably have higher birth rates, and that they maintain larger families after they have emigrated.

CLAIM:

Islamic belief leads to higher birth rates.

The greatest of all the strengths of radical Islam . . . is that it has demography on its side. The Western culture against which it has declared holy war cannot possibly match the capacity of traditional Muslim societies when it comes to reproduction. **- Niall Ferguson**

The sons of Allah . . . they multiply like rats. **- Orianna Falacci**

AS RECENTLY AS 1966, it was possible for a credible scholar to talk about an overall "Islamic fertility rate."[7] At the time, it seemed obvious that Islamic faith led to higher birth rates: the countries with Muslim majorities covered a swath of land suffering some of the world's most serious overpopulation. They had large families, and they'd always had large families. This, it seemed, was a product of immutable Islamic beliefs and family structures.

It is no longer possible to make such a claim. Consider the case of Iran. In the mid-1980s, the world's only Islamic theocracy had a fertility rate approaching 7 children per family. By 2010, Iranian average family sizes had fallen to 1.7 children—a lower rate than in Britain or France. This sharp fall was caused not by any religious change—Iranians remain devoutly Muslim—but by a rapid rate of urbanization, which is tied everywhere to smaller family sizes; by a very high level of education and literacy among women (which also correlates strongly with smaller family sizes); and by a high use of contraceptives (Islam does not feature Christianity's scriptural instruction to "multiply and replenish the Earth"). President Mahmoud Ahmadinejad, alarmed by the rising age and declining size of the population, launched a campaign in 2007 to urge Iranians to have more than 2 children per family. It had no effect: the birth rate kept shrinking.

Iran isn't alone. Turkey, governed for more than a decade by an elected party of Islamic believers, has seen its total fertility rate fall from 6 to 2.15. Even as Hezbollah gained influence in Lebanon, that country's rate fell to 1.86. Tunisia, leading a steep fall in fertility across Arab North Africa, now has a shrinking population, with 2.04 children per family. The United Arab Emirates has 1.9 children per family. Indonesia, the most populous Muslim country, now has a rate of 2.19, barely above the replacement rate, and is expected to fall below 2.0 by 2015; another South Pacific archipelago, Philippines, which is 90% Roman Catholic, has a fertility rate of 3.23. In the majority of Islamic countries, Muslim population growth rates are converging with those of Europe.

We should also look at the Muslims of Europe—not the post-1945 immigrants, but those who have lived there for more than half a millennium, in the former Ottoman countries of the Balkans. Albania, the continent's largest Muslim-majority country, has a non-growing fertility rate of 2 children per family, about the same as France's. Farther up the Adriatic coast, Bosnia's Muslims have one of the lowest fertility rates in the continent, with 1.23 children per family— a rate far lower than those of the country's Croatian and Serbian Christians. This gives the lie to the arguments by Bat Ye'or, Mark

Steyn and others that the Serbian-led war against Bosnian Muslims was the violent culmination of justifiable activism to prevent Bosnia becoming the bulwark of an imagined Muslim population invasion.

The fertility rate across all Muslim-majority countries has fallen from 4.3 children per family in 1995 to 2.9 in 2010, and is expected to fall by 2035 to 2.3 children, barely above the population-growth rate.[8] But it is true that some of the countries with the highest birth rates are Muslim: half of the 10 most fertile countries have Muslim majorities, including dire cases such as Afghanistan, with a 6.6 child-per-woman average, and Niger, with 7.2. And the majority of them are sub-Saharan states that are not physically far from the West, as several Eurabia authors note while suggesting that they will soon burst the shores of Africa and overwhelm Europe. But it is impossible to link those countries' Islamic beliefs and their birth rates, since fertility is equally high, and sometimes higher, among Christians and animists in these same countries. A study by American demographer Jennifer Johnson-Hanks finds that in "West African countries with Muslim majorities, Muslim fertility is lower than that of their non-Muslim co-nationals; in countries where Muslims are in the minority, their apparently higher reproductive rates converge to those of the majority when levels of education and urban residence are taken into account."[9] In other words, some Muslims have large families because they are poor, but neither the poverty nor the high fertility can be attributed to Islam—it is equally and sometimes even more present among other religions.

These countries with high birth rates produce very little immigration to Europe. The immigrants who do arrive in Europe soon conform, as we'll see below, to European fertility rates. Citing high Nigerian fertility rates as proof that Muslims will outnumber Europeans in their homelands is about as sensible as citing the high fertility rates of the Democratic Republic of the Congo, which is mainly Christian, as proof that Christians will outnumber Muslims in *their* homelands.

The French demographers Youssef Courbage and Emmanuel Todd, in a major study of Muslim fertility, literacy and population, concluded that there is no tie between Islamic beliefs and fertility rates, and that Muslim countries are undergoing one of the fastest rates of fertility decline in history. The drop in fertility in the Muslim world, Courbage concludes, "is concrete and powerful evidence that effectively destroys the Manichean idea of an unbridgeable divide between East and West and the idea that mentalities and behaviours have intangible religious roots."[10] It is true that traditional religious and agrarian societies have larger families. And many Islamic societies, especially those of the Middle East, held on to agrarian traditions longer than Western countries did, in part because of Arabic economic customs and family structures (such as marriage to cousins) that were at least partly a reflection of Islamic traditions. But demographers such as Courbage note that education of woman and urbanization have caused fertility to be "secularized"—that is, tied to individual choice rather than religious custom—across most Islamic societies. The fertility decline is most rapid and dramatic in the Muslim-majority countries that have the strongest immigration ties to the West. Globalization and immigration are not Islamifying the West, rather they are modernizing the Islamic countries that send immigrants westward. And if fertility rates in Islamic countries are fast converging with those of Europe and North America, we are left to ask what happens to those Muslims who become residents and citizens of the West. Are they really planting the seeds of massive population growth in their new host countries?

CLAIM:

Muslim immigrants in the West are destined to reproduce faster than the people around them.

Demographically, the enormous fertility of Muslim migrants is a threat to the cultural and civilizational equilibrium of an ageing Europe.
- Thilo Sarrazin

On the Continent and elsewhere in the West, native populations are aging and fading and being supplanted remorselessly by a young Muslim demographic . . . at the very minimum, this fast-moving demographic transformation provides a huge comfort zone for the jihad to move around in. **- Mark Steyn**

EVEN IF THERE'S no such thing as a Muslim fertility rate, it is true that immigrants have large families. Any social service agency will tell you that public-housing apartments built for four-person families are inadequate for big new-immigrant families. This is nothing new. Recently arrived immigrants have always had big families. As we shall see in chapter 3, the seemingly limitless issue of Roman Catholics and Jews in the neighbourhoods of Western cities was the subject of national hysteria throughout the nineteenth and twentieth centuries. But within a generation or two, their family sizes were little different from those of the general population.

Still we believe that Muslims are different: not only do they have larger families than the people around them, but they sometimes have higher fertility rates than their cousins back in the home country. Moroccan women in the Netherlands have a fertility rate of 2.9 children, while Moroccan women in Morocco have 2.4 children each. Bangladeshis in Britain have 3 children,[11] while those in Bangladesh have 2.4. So even if fertility rates at home are falling toward Western levels, relatives who have migrated to the West appear to be maintaining larger families. This, to some observers, is proof that there is a conspiracy of deliberate population growth, an invasion by reproductive means.

There are two important reasons for these higher numbers. First, the Muslim immigrants who come to Europe (though not so much to the United States or Canada) are overwhelmingly from rural areas, where fertility rates are much higher than the national average. Turks tend to come from rural Anatolia and the southeast, not from Istanbul or Ankara; Moroccans from the Rif mountains; the largest group of Pakistanis from Mirpur, a rural district in Kashmir; the majority of British Bangladeshis from Sylhet, an almost entirely rural district in the northeast of Bangladesh. Around the world and throughout history, rural families have more children—often many more. These immigrants aren't just changing from one national culture to another, but from a rural to an urban culture, which is an even more shocking adjustment. But it is a shift that universally leads to smaller families.[12] It also produces higher-than-usual levels of culture shock and insecurity—one of the key reasons why integration is slower and more difficult for some of these immigrants than it is for more urban immigrant groups.

Second, the highest family-size numbers are probably wrong. Women from Muslim countries tend to give birth to the majority of their children soon after arriving in their new homelands. Because of the way total fertility rate is calculated—by averaging the recorded births across a woman's fertile lifespan—a cluster of births will produce an exaggerated figure. We now have proof that this is occurring. A large-scale study from Germany shows that a sizable majority of immigrants from Turkey marry and have most of their children almost immediately after arrival.[13] Studies in France show that immigrant women tend to have children during their first two years in France—an effect that, once taken into account, lowers the real French Muslim fertility rate from 2.5 children to 2.2, barely above the native-born French rate. A similar effect is found in Sweden.[14]

This high birth rate in the early years tends to create a sense of panic among observers. It led to the rather startling observation, endlessly repeated in the Eurabia books, that the most common name for baby boys in Britain is Mohammed. This is true in some years (most recently 2010), if you count all 12 variants of its spelling as a single name, but it says little beyond the fact that Muslims have far less variety in their names than other, much larger ethnic groups—the majority of Muslim men in many cultures have Mohammed as their legal first name. At the same time, members of other ethnic groups (especially white Anglo-Saxons and black American Christians) are now more than 50% more likely than they were a generation before to give their children uncommon names.[15] The result is that Mohammeds can dominate the list without being terribly great in number: together, boys named after the prophet accounted for 1% of British newborns in 2010.[16]

That points to something else that lowers the population-growth rate. The Muslim immigrants in some countries supposedly being swamped by Islam are more likely to be male, as a result of immigration driven by manual-labour employment shortages that tend to attract unaccompanied men. Because intermarriage in the first generation is rare, few of these male immigrants are marrying and having offspring even if their community's fertility rate appears high. An average of 3 children per woman isn't as significant if only a third of your population is female. And that's exactly the case in Spain, which has 190 Moroccan men for every 100 Moroccan women. Italy has almost 160 Muslim men per 100 Muslim women. As the Pew study notes, "when a population has more men than women, the number of births tends to be lower than if the population is more balanced." The population growth for those Muslim communities will be nowhere near as high as the fertility rate suggests.[17]

But the vision of a Muslim tide isn't primarily based on immigrants having many children. It's based on *the children* of immigrants having many children, and their children having more children, and so on. Do the offspring of the Muslims who came to the West make babies at a Sudanese pace, or do they fall into the more modest childbearing patterns of Europe and North America? In short, do they become like the people around them?

France has the largest Muslim population in Western Europe, 4.7 million, and its politics are often defined by tensions over Islamic immigration. Many believe that the poor Muslim immigrants housed in the high-rise apartment towers on the edges of French cities have formed parallel societies, isolating themselves from the mainstream. The struggles of Muslims in France, including the 2005 riots, feature heavily in the Eurabia literature.

But French Muslims, despite their economic isolation, are falling fast into the reproduction patterns—and the cultural patterns—of their host country. A major study by American and French scholars found that fertility rates are "closely tied to length of residence in France . . . the longer immigrant women live in France, the fewer children they have; their fertility rate approaches that of native-born women." The real fertility rates of French Muslim women, as we have seen, are now only slightly higher than those of the general population, and they are still falling. The data, the authors conclude, "show that immigrants adapt to local norms (and, perhaps, to the cost of living) soon after arrival. The change may reflect acculturation, a reaction to living in close quarters, the entry of women into the workforce, or improved socioeconomic status."[18] This drop in fertility rate is a key measure of integration, and it is happening dramatically in France.

In Germany, home to more than 2 million Turkish immigrants and their children, the convergence has been even more remarkable. In 1970, Turks in Germany had 4.4 children each, and ethnic Germans 2. Today Turks have fewer than 2.2 children, barely above the general reproduction rate. Large-scale surveys suggest that the fertility rate of second-generation Turks is on the verge of falling to the very low German rate of 1.3 children. "Fertility of newly arriving immigrant cohorts will successively approach the low native level," an analysis of German birth statistics concludes.[19] Another study, using a large sample size and advanced methods, finds that among Muslims, "women of the second generation have nearly matched German women in their fertility patterns," having almost exactly the same number of children as non-Muslim Germans.[20] This sort of "fertility convergence" is not unique to Muslim immigrants; it is observed among other poor religious-minority immigrant groups, such as Latin American Catholics in the United States, whose birth rates are approaching those of the wider population, albeit slowly.[21]

Often characterized as the site of a Muslim demographic takeover, Austria is home to one of Europe's most extreme fertility contrasts: the Muslim population has a fairly high birth rate (2.3 to 2.4) and the non-Muslim population has an unusually low one (1.3). Several credible projections show that the Muslim population in Austria could come close to 10% by 2030 and could reach 14% to 18% by 2051 if immigration rates remain constant. This would make Islam the third-largest religion in Austria, by mid-century, behind Catholicism (which will fall just below 50% of the population). Atheists account for 34%.[22]

But before predicting that steeples will be driven out by minaret spires and Islam will reconquer Vienna by stealth (as several Eurabia authors have done), it's worth taking a closer look at what's happening. Austria's Muslims had a recorded fertility rate of 3.09 children per mother in 1981, 2.77 in 1991, and 2.3 in 2001: they have the fastest-falling fertility rates of any group in Austria. By 2030, that rate will fall to 2.1 children per family, not enough to create any growth; among non-Muslims, the rate is predicted to rise slightly to 1.4, leaving a very small gap. Indeed, one study projects that the fertility rates of Austria's Muslims will converge with those of non-Muslims shortly after 2030.[23]

Britain is headed, more slowly, in a similar direction. Its Muslim population comes mainly from Bangladesh and Pakistan, two countries whose fertility rates remain high. But the fertility rates of immigrants from those countries in Britain have fallen by half over the past 20 years, and the rates of their British-born children are considerably lower. Women living in Britain who emigrated from Pakistan have 3.5 children each, while their British-born daughters have 2.5. One study concludes that Pakistani and Bangladeshi immigrant fertility rates will drop to white British levels, depending on a number of hard-to-predict variables, between 2012 and 2040.[24] Canada, whose largest group of Muslim immigrants comes from the Indian subcontinent, will likely experience a similar pattern.

By 2030, even without any decrease in immigration levels, the Muslim and non-Muslim birth rates will be statistically identical in Germany, Greece, Spain and Denmark, and within half a child of one another in Belgium, France, Italy and Sweden. Across the entire European continent, the difference will be only 0.4, down from 0.7 two decades earlier. And that difference will continue to shrink.[25] At that rate, the continent's Muslims and non-Muslims should have nearly identical fertility rates by 2050.

This does not mean that those rates will converge in all countries. And growth can continue after the fertility rates become the same, because Muslims may have a larger population of childbearing age. But these trends do show that Muslims are following the path of earlier religious-minority immigrants to countries of the West, including Jews and Roman Catholics: from big families and rapid growth in the first couple of decades to a gradual blending into the fertility patterns of the host population later on. This fertility convergence, demographers note, is usually a strong indicator of other forms of integration. When women decide to have fewer children (for it is almost always their decision), it's a sign that their education levels and social values are falling into line with those of their new country.

Deprived of any genuine facts suggesting an overwhelming Muslim baby boom, the more radical Muslim-tide proponents simply make them up. More than 13 million people have now viewed the YouTube video "Muslim Demographics," which claims among other things that Germany will be a "Muslim state" by 2050. Every one of the video's claims is untrue. It says that French Muslims have 8.1 children and ethnic-French families 1.8 (the figures are 2.8 and 1.9, respectively). It says that a quarter of the Belgian population is Muslim (it's 6%), that the Netherlands will be half Muslim in 15 years (it will be 7.8% Muslim in 18 years)—and so on. For the core claims of "Muslim Demographics" to be true, Muslim immigrants in the West would need to have fertility rates far above the highest ever recorded in the world. As I've just shown, they're nowhere close. Tellingly, the video concludes by urging Christians to try to convert Muslims to their faith. Every one of its statistical claims has been thoroughly debunked,[26] but those claims appear to have been internalized by many viewers—including some writers and politicians who ought to know better. To these inflammatory stories of an Islamic baby boom, they have added the equally misleading tale of the coming deluge at our borders.

CLAIM:
In the future, a lot more immigration will be Muslim.

A youthful Muslim society to the south and east of the Mediterranean is poised to colonize—the term is not too strong—a senescent Europe.
- Niall Ferguson

But massive immigration from poor countries to rich ones is not a matter of a few criminal ringleaders breaking the rules of the game. It is the game, and there is no end to it in sight. The farther away Europe pushes the jumping-off point, the wider the orbit of those who consider themselves right next door . . . we fear they are in deadly, desperate earnest, and are staking their claim to a continent inhabited by people who are not. **- Christopher Caldwell**

TWO YEARS AFTER the collapse of the US subprime mortgage market triggered a set of economic and monetary calamities, the recession's impact reached the sun-blasted emptiness of the southeastern Atlantic Ocean. There, the ships from the European border agency Frontex that patrol the international waters off the Western Sahara for illegal immigrants suddenly found that they had become redundant: people just weren't jumping onto improvised rafts to flee to Europe anymore. Before 2008, patrols had tried to stop almost 32,000 people each year, the largest group of them Muslim, from making the often deadly voyage toward the Spanish territory of the Canary Islands. In 2009, that number dropped to around 7,000. By 2010, only 2,165 tried to come.[27] Altogether, illegal immigration levels across the European continent dropped by two-thirds.

In fact, at least 232,000 immigrants *left* Spain between 2008 and 2009 as jobs disappeared.

In the United States, the effect was even more dramatic. Immigration rates plummeted, and enough immigrants departed—not just to Latin America, but to Africa and elsewhere—that the total foreign-born population of the United States actually decreased, in 2008 and 2009, for the first time in its history.[28] Some observers called it a global immigration pause.

The recession's effect on immigration taught us two things. First, that immigrants—legal or illegal—don't take the risks and put out the cash to enter a foreign country simply in order to live there and collect welfare benefits. They come specifically to participate in the economy. Second, it taught us that, however tempting the metaphor, people do not actually pour out of poor overcrowded countries into the nearest prosperous states. Migration depends on cultural and economic connections. For instance, former colonial relationships cause Pakistanis, Indians and Bangladeshis to go mainly to Britain, and Algerians and Moroccans mainly to France. Turks don't pour into Bulgaria and Greece, or even Hungary and Slovakia, in any significant numbers but rather cross the Alps into Germany. They're not following an invasion path, but one of government-established economic connection.

Even refugees rarely flee to the nearest border: they take the risk of crossing multiple boundaries in order to get to the safest country. Iraqis who fled Saddam Hussein often went all the way to Australia. Migrants, even desperate ones, seek not the easiest journey for their families, but the most security at the end of it.[29] The people who leave the ultra-high-fertility West African states aren't desperately poor people fleeing in panic; they're people who have saved and then invested those savings in a careful, calculated decision. "Rather than a desperate response to destitution," the International Organization for Migration concluded in a study of such movements, "migration is generally a conscious choice by relatively well-off individuals and households to enhance their livelihoods." The numbers "fleeing" those countries are small: most years, refugees and asylum seekers make up little more than 5% of all international migration. Most immigration is for economic or family reasons. And Western countries aren't generally the destination of choice for poor African Muslims. The IOM study found that 62% to 80% of the 65,000 to 120,000 sub-Saharan Africans who head north each year are seeking work in North Africa.[30] Likewise, Middle Eastern Arabs are far more likely to migrate to Turkey or the wealthier states of the Persian Gulf; only a small minority seek entry to Europe.

In fact, if the West is being overwhelmed at all, it's not by Muslims. Despite its being "surrounded" by Islamic countries and sometimes having quite high immigration levels, Europe's proportion of Muslim immigrants is small. Though Spain is located across a narrow strait from the Arab world, only 13% of its immigrants each year are Muslims—the majority of both legal and illegal immigrants come from the other side of the Atlantic or from Romania, drawn by linguistic similarities. In Britain, only 28% of immigrants are Muslim; if a religious group is taking over in the United Kingdom, it is Roman Catholics, who passed Anglicans in church attendance decades ago.

In Germany, however intense the debate over Turks, fewer than 15% of immigrants are Muslim—a far larger group comes from Eastern Europe. In fact, France is the only European country whose immigrants are largely Muslim (68.5%), in large part because many of them were French citizens a generation ago, when Algeria and Tunisia were French territory.[31] Furthermore, the Muslim proportion of immigration is not growing and it seems unlikely to do so in the future. The "Arab Spring" revolutions of 2011 did not produce the large increase of cross-Mediterranean immigration the media had predicted; beyond a small initial group of refugees in the early months of the year, those uprisings coincided with a period of decreasing immigration from the region.[32]

The migrant-packed urban districts of Belgium, the Netherlands and Scandinavia that became the subject of so many Eurabia books are today becoming populated with a new wave of Poles, Romanians and Russians. Indeed, anti-Muslim politicians such as Geert Wilders have begun to shift the focus of their anxiety to the new Slavic tide. Immigration is not a Muslim monopoly, and certainly not an Islamic plot. But because Muslims are often very visible, and often more controversial than other migrants, they may seem to be far more numerous than they really are. And, sometimes, their presence leads us to suspect that there must be something wrong with us.

CLAIM:

An atheist, socialist, welfare-dependent West has lost the moral will to reproduce and to resist an Islamic takeover.

The spiritual tawdriness Islamic immigrants perceive in the modern West is not imaginary. It may be Europe's biggest liability in preserving its culture. . . . When an insecure, malleable, relativistic culture meets a culture that is anchored, confident, and strengthened by common doctrines, it is generally the former that changes to suit the latter.
- Christopher Caldwell

This is about . . . the larger forces at play in the developed world that have left Europe too enfeebled to resist its remorseless transformation into Eurabia and that call into question the future of much of the rest of the world. The key factors are: demographic decline; the unsustain-ability of the social democratic state; and civilizational exhaustion . . . . Islam has youth and will, Europe has age and welfare. **- Mark Steyn**

HAVE ATHEISM AND the welfare state caused the West to collapse into infertile decline, leaving its empty, faithless cities open to takeover by determined Islamic believers? This is one of the most popular claims of Muslim-tide authors, who argue that the most spiritually weak, socialistic and infertile countries of the West are falling prey to Islamic dominance. As it happens, this is a fairly easy hypothesis to test. You just need to examine the numbers.

First, look at a list of the most religious countries in the West (as measured by the percentage of the population who attend a house of worship regularly).[33] Right up in the top rank, below only Ireland, is Poland, whose rate of regular church attendance is 55%, more than twice the world average of 26%. Next come Slovakia (47%), Portugal (47%), and Italy (45%). Other surveys show very high religious observance in Malta (75%).[34] In all of these countries, religion plays a large, visible part in public and political life.

Now examine the European countries with the lowest fertility rates, and the fastest-shrinking and fastest-aging populations. You're essentially looking at the same list. In the top 10 are Poland (only 1.3 children per family), Slovakia (1.3), Malta (1.3), Portugal (1.4) and Italy (1.4). The most religious countries in Europe are also, generally, those with the most acute fertility failure. The lone exception is Ireland, which has both high church attendance and a high birth rate. Otherwise, there is a direct correlation between the most religious and the least fertile countries.

On the other hand, the most fertile states in Europe include France (1.97 children), Iceland (2.1), Denmark (1.8), Norway (1.9) and Sweden (1.9)*—every one of them either a Scandinavian social democracy or a big-spending welfare state. These also happen to be among the countries with the highest rates of atheism and the lowest rates of religious observance. Britain is also on the list, with a non-Muslim fertility rate of 1.8 children and one of the lowest religious-observance rates in the world. If something is hollowing out Europe and leaving it vulnerable to immigrant population growth, it sure isn't secularism or the nanny state: those factors, if anything, are acting as remedies.

And Muslim immigrants are not settling in the declining countries with low fertility rates, such as Portugal or Slovakia. Rather, they are moving to fast-reproducing countries such as France, Britain and Sweden, or to economically booming places like Germany. Keep in mind those earlier figures showing that immigrants generally arrive only when countries are experiencing economic success. Which hypothesis seems more likely: that Muslim immigrants are taking advantage of weak, defenceless, fading societies in order to impose themselves, or that Muslim immigrants are coming to the strongest and most appealing societies they can find and trying hard to become members? Western countries don't attract people because of their failings and shortcomings—they attract people because of their successes.

---

* These countries all appear near the top of the European fertility-rate list even if you subtract Muslim immigrants from their totals. France's non-Muslims have a high rate of 1.9 children, Norway's and Sweden's 1.8, and the rest have fertility rates that are unchanged without Muslims.

II INTEGRATION

THE MUSLIM NEIGHBOURHOODS of the West do not look like other urban districts. In some ways they resemble outposts of the Middle East and North Africa: bearded men drinking coffee and smoking shisha pipes on the sidewalk, women in head coverings, the strict observance of Islamic customs such as the sacrifice of sheep at the beginning of Eid al-Adha, and the looming presence of the mosque. Given the defiant points of the minarets and the forest of satellite dishes receiving signals from faraway lands, it is hard to avoid thinking that these people are receiving their instructions from somewhere else. Do the Muslim families in our midst have any interest in becoming part of our society, or do they believe themselves to be part of another society entirely? Do they support our institutions and values, or are they interested in importing and establishing other, less desirable ones? Or are these rough neighbourhoods simply the latest version of the grand narrative of immigration, earlier iterations of which have left us drinking espresso and dotting our language with Yiddish expressions, but otherwise unperturbed by the variety of religious customs in our midst?

CLAIM:

Muslim immigrants are overwhelmingly guided by a religion that they regard as more an ideology than a spiritual faith.

While there are such things as moderate and liberal Christianity, there is no such thing as a moderate or liberal Islam. . . . Today, rather, Islam remains overwhelmingly a totalizing ideology—one whose edicts encompass all of life and are highly specific and severe in regard to adherents' belief and conduct. **- Bruce Bawer**

I see Islam not so much as a religion as much as an ideology. As I see it, the aim of the Islamic ideology is to dominate and to submit the Western societies to their belief, and this is unlike the other religions. I say that Islam is not another branch on the tree of religions—it has to be put in the corner of totalitarian ideologies. **- Geert Wilders**

EVEN IF THOSE WORRIED about the Muslim tide accept the numbers and realize that Muslims are unlikely to become more than 10% of the population in the countries of the West, they will continue to argue that these immigrants' strong, intolerant religious beliefs will make them a disruptive bloc. This is a community, they will argue, of perpetually illiberal zealots whose adherence to the Koran puts them at odds with Western values and whose inevitable cultural backwardness makes them a threat to the West's hard-fought progress toward sexual and gender equality and freedom of belief.

All manner of claims are used to support this argument: that the Koran is received as divine, unchangeable revelation rather than a human account open to interpretation; that various passages from the Koran present Islam as a philosophy of state rather than of individual motive; that many imams present total adherence as the only option open to a believer; and that Islam, as presented in scripture, does not allow for the possibility of multiple interpretations, of moderate or reformist schools, or of a separate secular sphere of thought.

The problem with this argument is that religions do not manifest themselves in scripture or dogma, they manifest themselves in human behaviour. Even among the devout, behaviour is often dramatically at odds with scripture. Judaism is, on paper, a closed and hermetic faith that denies the possibility of Reform or liberal interpretations, or the fact that many Jews today are non-religious. Christianity, as any fundamentalist will tell you, commands its followers to place the laws of God (as revealed in scripture) above those of man, even if there is a price to be paid for disobeying the latter. Roman Catholics are not given the option of selectively obeying the teachings of the Church; nevertheless, the overwhelming majority of the Church's adherents in the West are decidedly "cafeteria Catholics" who pick and choose the teachings that suit their lifestyle.

Are Muslim immigrants in the West practising a "buffet-table Islam" suited to the values around them? Are they picking up the values of the West, or are they singular Islamic believers who just happen to be living in the West?

One approach to finding this out is simply to ask. Another is to gauge Muslim opinions and actions in areas of morality and behaviour that force them to choose between a religious or a civic view of the world. Luckily, the last few years have seen some of the most internationally respected survey organizations conduct large-scale investigations of Muslim opinion and behaviour in Western countries. Many have concentrated on questions of religious versus national loyalty.

We'll begin in France, where 4 in 10 citizens feel that "most immigrants have a culture too distinct from French to be able to integrate into French society."[35] And indeed, immigrants to France from Muslim lands do tend to identify themselves by their religious faith more than other French citizens do—but far less than citizens of Muslim countries do. In 2006, 42% of French Muslims said they felt "French first and Muslim second," while 46% felt Muslim first. Since the same survey found that between 77% and 79% of Muslims living in Arab states see themselves as Muslim first, this marks a sharp shift from religious to national identity after immigrating.[36] Still, it means that some Muslim immigrants in France (only half of whom have become full citizens) remain more inclined to identify themselves by their religion. Does this religious identity shape their beliefs and actions? Here, France's secular practices seem to have had a dramatic influence on Muslims.

Whatever their self-identity, France's 4.7 million Muslims are largely non-practising: French government studies indicate that 8% to 15% regularly attend religious services, and that fewer than 5% attend a mosque every Friday—similar to the 9% of French Catholics who attend mass once a week.[37] In fact, 20% of French people from Muslim backgrounds said they have no religion at all—not that far below French adults in general, 28% of whom report they have no religion. And among those with religion, 28% of Muslims said they "never prayed," versus 38% of religious Catholics. Almost no French Muslims send their children to separate Islamic schools, despite a 2004 French law banning the display of religious symbols, including the Muslim hijab, in public-school classrooms. In fact, 42% of French Muslims said they *support* this ban.[38] By any measure, these immigrants have decided to engage with their religion in a way that is distinctly French.

It's interesting to contrast these French findings with statistics from the United States. There, 49% of immigrants from Muslim backgrounds say they consider themselves Muslim first and American second. And 69% say that religion is "very important in their lives," while fully 47% claim to attend a mosque every Friday, many times the rate we found in France.

But these figures are nearly identical to trends among Americans in general, who tend to be quite religious: 46% of all American Christians (and 70% of evangelicals) say they identify themselves as "Christian first" and American second. And 70% of Christians—a higher proportion than Muslims—say that religion is "very important in their lives," while 45% attend a church service every Sunday. In other words, American Muslims have adopted almost exactly the same level of religious observance and identification as their American Christian counterparts. In matters of scriptural interpretation, just 37% of US Muslims say there is "only one true interpretation" of their religion, not far above the rate of US Christians, 28% of whom believe there is only one way to interpret the Bible's teachings. And 63% of American Muslims say there is "no conflict between being a devout Muslim and living in modern society"— compared to the 64% of American Christians who say the same of their religion.[39]

Rather extraordinarily, fully 62% of American Muslims say that "a way can be found for the state of Israel to exist so that the rights of Palestinians are addressed"—a rate many times higher than Muslims polled in the Middle East. The rate is not much lower than that of Americans in general, 67% of whom support that statement. Only 16% of US Muslims, and 12% of US citizens in general, believe that Israel's existence prevents Palestinians from having rights. By contrast, 80% of Egyptians and Jordanians, 45% of Turks and 59% of Lebanese believe it does. So even on the explosive issue of Palestinian-Israeli relations, Muslim immigrants are abandoning the views of their home countries and falling into the American mainstream.[40]

Despite their proximity to the Arab world, French Muslims also seem to have fallen in line with their country's popular view of the Middle East. While polls find that a small majority of French residents with an Arab or Turkish background have a negative image of Israel (52%), this percentage is actually *lower* than the average French response (55%).[41]

It's not just politics: on any number of issues where we would expect religious doctrine to guide the opinions of Muslim immigrants, the local culture of their new countries holds sway. On homosexuality, for example. In the United States, 39% of Muslims said in 2009 that homosexuality should be accepted. While this is lower than the 58% acceptance rate among the general American public, it is an increase on the response of 27% given by US Muslims four years earlier. Of Muslims who were born in the United States, 41% accept homosexuality. This represents a very rapid rate of integration on an issue that has been described as an emblem of civilizational division by Muslim-tide writers and politicians such as Bruce Bawer and Geert Wilders.

Muslims in Germany have become even more tolerant of homosexuality, with 47% of German Muslims (versus 68% of Germans in general) finding it morally acceptable, according to a large-scale Gallup survey. This is despite the fact that German Muslims, generally Turkish and rural in origin, are among the most religious in Europe, with 82% saying religion is "an important part of my daily life" (compared with 70% in Britain and 69% in France). The Gallup poll also found that 48% of French Muslims find sex between an unmarried man and woman morally acceptable, and 35% tolerate abortion—rather extraordinary opinions for French Arabs, a majority of whom were born in North Africa.[42] Among American Muslims, 90% feel that women should be allowed to work outside the home, and 7 out of 10 feel there is no difference between male and female political leaders—views little different from those of all Americans, and a world away from those held in the countries they and their parents came from.[43]

In general, while their values still lag behind those of their non-immigrant neighbours, and that discrepancy is the source of considerable tension, immigrants of Muslim origin are very clearly progressing toward integration at a rapid pace—especially when you consider that the largest group of these immigrants has arrived in the last 20 years. Moreover, it took Europeans and North Americans decades to build the beginnings of legal and social consensus behind women's rights, homosexual equality and birth control. Muslim immigrants, coming from a far lower level of economic development, appear to be adopting those views much more rapidly.

THERE ARE, HOWEVER, exceptions to this pattern of cultural integration. A notable one is Britain, where the views of Muslim immigrants are, on average, starkly different from those of the wider country. While 58% of Britons accept homosexuality, the Gallup pollsters found almost no British Muslims who expressed tolerance (other polls have shown around 20% Muslim tolerance of homosexuality in the United Kingdom). More British Muslims were opposed to abortion (only 5% of Muslims in the United Kingdom tolerated it, compared with 19% of German and 35% of French Muslims) and to sex between unmarried partners (only 3% of British Muslims accept it). And only in Britain are Muslim women more likely to stay at home: in 2004, 69% of them were "economically inactive," compared with 40% of all non-Christian women in Britain and 25% of Christian women. (Only 30% of Muslim men in Britain were "economically inactive").[44] While a great many Bangladeshis and Pakistanis are active in public life, politics and academia in Britain, a majority are not adopting modern or European views anywhere near as quickly as their French or German counterparts. Some attribute this trend to British multiculturalism policies that encouraged self-segregation in northern cities where unemployment is high; others see it as the lingering influence of their very conservative, rural home societies in Pakistan and Bangladesh.

Gallup has developed an index of integration that uses a complex series of questions to measure attitudes toward, and interactions with, people of other religions. People strongly able to coexist with other communities and religions are classed as "integrated," those oblivious to or intolerant of other groups are "isolated," and those in the middle are "tolerant." By this measure, French Muslims are the most integrated, with 46% of respondents meeting that test, compared with 22% of the French general public. Only 10% of British Muslims are "integrated." The vast majority of them (60%), though, are not "isolated" but merely "tolerant," which means they have a live-and-let-live view of the wider community but often fail to see the merits of it. This, on the face of it, seems to show that some Muslim groups, most dramatically those in Britain, do not have an interest in integrating in important ways, at least not quickly. But do their loyalties lie elsewhere, in the Koran or in some other country's values?

That question requires a different analysis.

CLAIM:

Muslim immigrants are not loyal to their host countries. Their loyalties lie with their religion or their countries of birth.

Today, at the dawn of the twenty-first century, a conflict of civilizations is reemerging on European soil in the context of Islamic immigration. . . . Numerous Muslims have successfully adapted to Western democracy, but they are still the exceptions. Preachers in mosques continue to . . . request Muslims to educate their children in the spirit of jihad. **- Bat Ye'or**

Imagine that the West, at the height of the Cold War, had received a mass inflow of immigrants from Communist countries who were ambivalent about which side they supported. . . . Something similar is taking place now. **- Christopher Caldwell**

SOME MUSLIM GROUPS ARE integrating into their host cultures with amazing rapidity, while others are lagging behind. The question is whether the laggards are actively rejecting the values of their new countries out of alienation or disloyalty, or simply staying on the margins because they lack the knowledge or resources to fit in. Are they outsiders, angry at the nation around them and seeking to turn it into something else? Or are they merely citizens who are temporarily clinging to older patterns of life?

Those British Muslims with their conservative values are a good test case. A 2009 Gallup survey of opinions held by minorities in European countries found that "British Muslims *are more likely than all populations surveyed* to identify strongly with their nation, and to express stronger confidence in its democratic institutions." This was not a subtle difference: fully 77% of British Muslims say they identify "extremely strongly" or "very strongly" with their country, versus only 50% of Britons in general, 52% of French Muslims, and 40% of German Muslims.[45]

Among Britain's various religious and secular communities, it is the Muslims who feel the strongest affinity for the state—and the greatest optimism about it. In a study of national pride conducted in 2011 by the London research organization Demos, researchers found that 83% of Muslims said they were "proud to be a British citizen"—a higher rate than for Britons in general (79%). And only 31% of Muslims agreed that "Britain's best days are behind her," versus 45% of the general population and 50% of Anglicans. "Overall," the report concluded, "British Muslims are more likely to be both patriotic and optimistic about Britain than are the white British community."[46] Note that these Muslims aren't simply happy to have British citizenship: they personally identify with the British nation in its current state and express support for the existing function of its institutions.

This distinction is verified in other large-scale surveys. When the Open Society Institute studied the views of Muslim minorities in 11 European cities,[47] it found that those most likely to see themselves as citizens of their nations (that is, as British or French rather than as Muslims, Bangladeshis, Arabs and so on) were living in Leicester (82% identified first as "British") and London (72%).* While the lack of British Muslim-immigrant integration on social

---

* Other cities where Muslims strongly saw themselves as national citizens first include Amsterdam (59%), Marseille (58%) and Antwerp (55%); this identity was held by a minority of Muslims in Hamburg (22%), Berlin (25%), Copenhagen (40%), Paris (41%), Stockholm (41%) and Rotterdam (43%).

and sexual matters is worrying, it is clearly not rooted in a lack of loyalty to Britain or in alienation from the Western institutions of national life.

The same study found that 73% of Muslim immigrants to Europe who are eligible to vote had participated in national elections, only slightly below the rate of the general population (81%)—and that Muslim women were just as likely to vote as men. And half of Muslims said they had been involved in some form of civic participation through "mixed organizations rather than organizations based on their own ethnicity or religion."[48]

In France, Muslims often appear to be the most enthusiastic backers of the state. One study found that 62% of Muslims feel that "democracy is functioning well in France" versus 58% of the general population; another study asking the same question got responses of 69% versus 58%, with Muslims giving a 95% overall favourability rating to France and its institutions.[49] And a major poll of French Muslims conducted by the US State Department in 2005—after the headscarf ban and the riots by Muslim immigrants in the Paris suburbs—concluded that "large majorities of Muslims in France voice confidence in the country's government, feel at least partly French, and support integrating into French society."[50]

In their daily lives, the Muslims of France hardly seem to be taking instruction from the pages of the Koran or from foreign imams. In less than two generations, the fertility rate of Muslim immigrants has fallen to close to the rate of native-born French citizens. French rather than Arabic is almost universally spoken by immigrants. A 2005 poll found that 8 in 10 Muslims were "comfortable with people of different religions dating or marrying" and 59% would not object to their daughter marrying a non-Muslim[51]—something that appears to be happening, as a quarter of French Muslim women are married to non-Muslim men and 50% of young Muslim men are cohabiting with a non-Muslim woman.[52] Sixty percent of French Muslims say they have "many French friends"; 45% say they have at least some Jewish friends. And in an important indication of cultural integration, 57% of Muslim women in France are employed outside the home—a rate not much lower than for French women (63%) and very different from rates of female employment in the Arab states that send immigrants to France.

While there are still incidents of Muslim immigrants protesting against the societies around them—most recently seen in the string of riots and attacks against the 2005 Danish newspaper cartoons featuring the Prophet Mohammed, and earlier in mass protests against the Iraq War—it is now just as likely that Western Muslims will take action to defend their adopted societies and governments, as Muslims did in the August 2011 riots in English cities. In that eruption of violence,* Pakistani- and Bangladeshi-origin Britons overwhelmingly served as defenders of property; three of the five deaths were Birmingham Muslims killed while protecting buildings against rioters. It is no longer surprising to see Muslim immigrants and their children in the highest ranks of European public life. The chairwoman of Britain's Conservative Party is the daughter of Pakistani immigrants; the leader of Germany's third most popular party, the Greens, is a Turkish immigrant; and several members of former French president Nicolas Sarkozy's first cabinet were Muslims. Contrasting these immigration success stories, though, are sizable numbers of Muslims who remain poor and culturally isolated, especially in Europe. Are they are choosing this isolation or having it thrust on them?

---

* Court reports show that 93% of those arrested for rioting were white or black, and only 7% were "Asian or mixed Asian," the usual British designation for Muslims, Hindus and Sikhs.

CLAIM:

Muslim immigrants want to live apart, in isolated "parallel societies."

Muslims are more likely to live in tightly knit religious communities, to adhere to a narrow fundamentalist faith, and to resist integration into mainstream society. . . . [In the Netherlands], most people of non-Dutch origin are fundamentalist Muslims, and most, even after years or decades in Europe, remain largely unintegrated. **- Bruce Bawer**

Muslims not only despise western secular values as decadent, materialistic, corrupt and immoral, they do not accept the distinction between the spiritual and the temporal, the division which in Christian societies confines religion to the margins of everyday life. Instead, for Muslims the whole of human life must represent a submission to God. This means that they feel a duty to Islamicise the values of the surrounding culture.
- Melanie Phillips

MOST MUSLIM IMMIGRANTS come from poor, culturally conservative countries that are often economically isolated from the larger world. Many come from impoverished rural districts within those countries. When they come to the West, they often make their start in Muslim-dominated urban neighbourhoods or public-housing blocks that are rife with poverty, unemployment, petty crime and welfare dependency. This is true of most poor immigrants, but Muslims tend to attract extra attention. Many observers believe that they are ghettoizing themselves into parallel societies and have no interest in integrating with the wider society and economy around them.

As the polling data above demonstrate, Muslim immigrants in most countries are adapting quickly to the social and sexual values and fertility patterns of the West, and they are generally becoming enthusiastic supporters of the state and democratic institutions around them. But people still worry that in other important ways they aren't fitting in—perhaps because they don't want to—and that they are raising their children to be part of a separate Muslim society, not the larger national one. The charge is that Muslim immigrants deliberately stay within Islamic enclaves, refusing to teach their children the languages of the host country and creating Arabic or Asian villages inside our cities.

It's unquestionably true that many Muslim immigrants are impoverished and isolated from the mainstream economy. For example, a recent review of the labour-market integration of ethnic minorities in Belgium, Denmark, the Netherlands and Britain found that they "typically have significantly higher unemployment rates, lower labour income, and they are less likely to find and keep their jobs than the majority population."[53] The proportion of the population of Belgium living below the poverty line is 10% for native Belgians, 59% for Turkish immigrants and 56% for Moroccan immigrants. In Amsterdam, 32% of Turkish households and 37% of Moroccan households live on the minimum income, compared with 13% of Dutch households.[54]

In Britain, a study of immigrant poverty by the Joseph Rowntree Foundation found that 65% of Bangladeshis and 55% of Pakistanis are poor, compared with 20% of "White British" people. Twenty-five percent of Pakistani households and 30% to 35% of Bangladeshi households are "workless" (that is, with nobody in the household who is employed), while the rate for white British households is around 15%. Meanwhile, those Muslims who do have work receive much lower average compensation than other immigrant groups. Almost half of Bangladeshi workers and a third of Pakistanis were paid less than £6.50 per hour in 2006 (the minimum wage is £6.08), compared with a fifth of the other ethnic immigrants. (This was partly because it was found that 35% of Bangladeshis, compared with 5% of other ethnic groups, were employed in the "hotels and catering sector"— that is, mainly in family-owned curry restaurants, which are often instruments of social mobility, despite their low pay.)[55]

In the 11 European cities studied by the Open Society Institute, Muslims "are not integrated into the mainstream labour market." They faced more joblessness, lower pay and greater vulnerability to layoffs. While some of this disadvantage was accounted for by poor language fluency and lack of knowledge or understanding of the labour market, a gap still remained that the researchers attributed to "an ethnic and a religion penalty in the labour market."

And that is the key to understanding the impoverished state of these immigrants: they are not choosing to be poor and on welfare, but most often are forced into it. We know this, in part, because it is not the fate of Muslim immigrants alone. Poverty currently afflicts all visible minority immigrant groups who came to the West as unskilled, semiskilled or working-class labourers. One Europe-wide analysis of employment and poverty found that, once differences in education were accounted for, "ethnic penalties" created serious dis-advantages for workers not just from Turkey, Morocco and Pakistan, but equally for those from the Caribbean (largely Christian) and Suriname (mainly Christian and Hindu).[56]

In Canada, a major analysis of national statistics found that skin colour, not religion, affected the ability to integrate, and that Muslims are no less (and sometimes slightly more) able to integrate economi-cally and socially than other people of the same race. "Consistent with their membership in visible minority groups," the research con-cluded, "Muslims, Hindus, Sikhs, and Buddhists experience more disadvantage both objectively in terms of household income and subjectively in terms of reported discrimination and vulnerability. . . . Overall, it seems clear that religion, particularly Islam, is not a decisive factor affecting social integration when religious differences are examined among visible minority groups. If anything, South Asian and Arab and West Asian Muslims report somewhat higher levels of integration than co-ethnics in other religions."[57]

Aside from demonstrating that the problems of isolation and economic exclusion are not unique to Muslims, a large body of research also shows that Muslim emigrants from the same countries of origin have very different fates depending on which country they choose as their destination. In some places, they become fully integrated within a generation; in others, they and their children seem to become trapped on the margins. This is significant, because it means that the immigrants are not isolating themselves from society by choice, or out of religion or ideology, but rather because some host countries fail to provide the necessary means for acculturation and inclusion.

The American economist Jacob Vigdor analyzed the integration of Muslim immigrants in nine countries and produced an index—measured by rates of male and female employment, home ownership and naturalization—meant to gauge to what extent immigrants from Muslim countries have become part of their new host countries. Canada's "assimilation index" ranked the highest, at 77 out of a possible 100, with very high scores in all categories except female employment. The United States came close to Canada with a score in the 60s, but Muslims in European countries lagged far behind, with assimilation rates ranging from Spain's 38 to Italy's 11. Those rates were pulled down, he found, not by cultural factors but by very poor rates of home ownership and naturalization. The pathway to full legal citizenship and ownership of property is blocked by restrictive laws in too many European countries—and it may be this, rather than religion or alienation, that prevents many Muslim immigrants from participating fully in the economy.[58]

And if the Muslim immigrants are victims of barriers beyond their control, their native-born children are even more so. This second generation tends to have values and behaviours that come very close to those of the native population. But their ability to integrate fully depends heavily on the education system—and here there can be problems.

In North America, Muslims are educational successes, with attainment levels among the best of any ethnic group. In the United States, 40% of adult Muslims have earned a college degree or a more advanced degree, making them the second most educated religious group after Jews (61%), and far ahead of average Americans (29%).[59]

But this is not the case in most of Europe, in part because Muslims typically emigrated to fill unskilled-labour shortages in the host countries and therefore start out with greater educational shortcomings. Also, European school systems are ill designed to provide educational advantages to immigrant children. Children of migrants in many European countries have far higher secondary-school dropout rates, and they are shunted at high rates into vocational secondary-school streams rather than university-bound streams.[60] In Germany, children of Turkish descent are more than twice as likely as Germans to be directed to a *Hauptschule*, the lowest of the secondary education tracks; barely more than 10% of them are permitted to attend a *Gymnasium*. As a result, Turkish students are more than twice as likely as Germans to leave school without a diploma.[61]

The students' success or failure, however, wasn't determined by their membership in an ethnic or religious group, but rather by the school and the education system they happened to attend. Immigrants from the same country will fare extremely well in one

European state's education system, and in another will drop out early. "The educational attainment of migrant students is comparatively high in countries with a well developed system of preschool education and rather late selection of students to different tracks (ability grouping) of the education system," a European study concludes. "Education systems with a high degree of selectivity also work to the disadvantage of migrant children and youth." In other words, when school structures and curricula are designed with a plural society and multispeed learning in mind—as is most often the case in Britain, Canada and the United States, but still rare in continental Europe—the children of Muslim immigrants tend to have levels of educational achievement close to those of the general population.[62]

The bottom line is that these children are often suffering not from Islam—or ethnicity or even immigration status—but rather from low income. Muslim-immigrant children have the same disappointing results in school and employment as children of native-born parents in similar income groups; in fact, many do somewhat better. "Children of immigrants," as one study in France found, "do as well as or better in their course work than children of French parents of the same socioeconomic class."[63] Unfortunately, two-thirds of immigrant children in France are earning working-class incomes or lower.

In every European country, if you compare children of Muslim immigrants with average children, they typically appear to be faring poorly in school. But if you compare them with children from families with the same low incomes, the gap often narrows or disappears.[64] In Britain, it actually reverses: in comparisons of the academic performance of students eligible for free school meals (an indicator of poverty), Pakistani and Bangladeshi students perform significantly better than their white British counterparts. In the public-housing estates of East London, it is the Muslim-immigrant kids (especially the girls) who are the most likely to go to university, get a job and move out of the neighbourhood, leaving their ethnic-English neighbours behind.[65] Statistics show that, while new immigrants from Muslim countries receive considerably less education than other people in their host countries, their children narrow the gap. French-born Muslim children receive about the same number of years of education as ethnic-French kids, German-born Muslims receive on average only 1.9 years less education, and British-born Muslims receive an average of 1 year *more* education than white British kids.[66] These are averages, though, and they can hide a wide discrepancy within those groups.

There are three dynamics at work here: the almost universal immigrant drive to succeed and to produce a better outcome for your children; the inability of these very poor immigrant families to engage with the school system and understand how education works in the West; and a school system that tends to shunt poor immigrant children into the same low-skill, low-education trajectories as their parents. The result is that children of Muslim immigrants either exceed or fail, but are rarely average.

In the Netherlands, for example, second-generation children appear to be splitting into two groups. Those who drop out of secondary school, at a rate more than twice the national average, are very likely to fall into unemployment and benefit dependency. Of the smaller group who stay in school, more than 40% end up in higher education (though more often in technical colleges than universities). A large-scale Dutch study of second-generation success found that there is "a considerable group that stays behind and an equally large group that performs remarkably well."[67] This is the same pattern we see in Britain: Pakistani and Bangladeshi young people are overrepresented among those entering higher education, and at the same time over-represented among those leaving school without qualifications.[68] In other words, there is a polarization *within* ethnic groups—something we've seen in other groups of poor immigrants. This is, in a way, reassuring. It means that Muslim immigrants are on the path once followed by other religious-minority immigrants, and encountering the same mix of opportunities and obstacles. But it also means that many school systems are failing them.

Worse, Muslim immigrants who do complete a good education and seek a place in Western society can encounter devastating barriers. One study of four European countries found that the higher-than-average educational achievements of many Muslims are reversed as soon as they try to enter the workforce. While their parents (the new immigrants) earn far less than natives do, their children, the second-generation Muslims, who have the same language fluency and have achieved levels of education that are the same or better than those of the native population, do not manage to narrow the wage gap. British-born Bangladeshis do twice as well as their parents in the labour market—but that is still far worse than British-born Britons. German-born Turks actually earn *less* than their Turkish-born parents, despite having more years of education.[69] As a study of the children of immigrants in Britain concluded, "British born ethnic minority individuals, despite having more schooling, have lower employment probabilities than their British born white peers . . . [and] obtain lower wages on average for the same observable characteristics."[70] Or, as the Open Society Institute study concluded, "Human capital accounts for some of this disadvantage; other factors include social networks, knowledge and understanding of the labour market and language fluency." But even after all that has been taken into account, it appears that children of Muslim immigrants face "both an ethnic and a religion penalty in the labour market."[71]

Most Muslim immigrants do not lack the desire to integrate or to become full members of the economic and educational community in their new countries. There does seem to be a group of young males who are leaving school early and failing to find an economic place in the postindustrial economies of the West—something they have in common with the sons and grandsons of the white working class in many European countries. They are certainly a worry. It ought to be a major project of European education departments to create incentives and systems to keep these second-generation men in education, training and employment, since their disenfranchisement will create larger and more expensive problems in the future. But they are outnumbered by a far larger group who are trying hard to succeed, but often running headlong into barriers in schooling and employment that seem designed to keep them out.

What we have, in the end, is a poor but ambitious community, making a tough adjustment from rural to urban life across national and often linguistic boundaries. They are no more religious than earlier waves of poor immigrants and are mainly seeking inclusion into the world of education and work. Those who fall out and become isolated or perpetually poor are not inevitable products of their community but generally victims of gaps and flaws in our economic and educational systems. For the most part, they exhibit no signs of any desire to become a "parallel society," either culturally or economically—but there are circumstances that could be creating one by default.

III EXTREMISM

THAT IS ALL WELL and good, you might reasonably say, but what about the suicide bombers? Whatever the progress made by Muslim immigrants, however illusory the demographic threat, there remains the undeniable fact of jihadist terrorism. The violent Islamic extremism of this century's first decade was largely a phenomenon within the Islamic world, and the great majority of its victims were Muslim. Still, there were enough violent incidents committed by homegrown radicals in the West—enough innocents killed in the London Underground and at Fort Hood, Texas—and enough terrorist cells intercepted while plotting attacks in Western countries to make even liberal-minded people wonder if the arrival of millions of Muslims from the east and south carried this wave of violence as its inevitable consequence.

Are these moments of violence the product of a distinct political movement rooted in notions of religious segregation, or the result of a wider anger and a more popular system of belief? Do significant numbers of ordinary Muslims subscribe to a set of spiritual and cultural ideals that put them perpetually at odds with the majority in the West? If so, it is possible that any reasonably faithful believer, or loyal member of the Islamic community, could decide to take to the streets, or take up arms, in opposition to the world around them. On the other hand, if the jihadist wave is a self-contained political movement with no relation to the wider faith or community in which it resides—something more akin to the anticapitalist terror attacks committed by circles of middle-class Germans, Americans and Italians in the 1970s or the separatist violence carried out by the Irish in North America and Britain in the nineteenth and twentieth centuries—then it needs to be confronted differently, as a criminal tendency that is as much a threat to the wider Muslim community as it is to anyone else.

One type of violence is self-contained, criminal and transitory. The other is endemic, widespread and inevitable. To understand which kind we're facing, we need to examine the motives of the violent few, as well as those of the wider immigrant community.

CLAIM:

Muslims in the West tend to be angry at the society around them.

As has become evident of late, a vast number of Muslims, those living in Europe and the Americas no less than those elsewhere, harbor an intense hostility to the West. **- Daniel Pipes**

Islam, like other religions, has also known periods when it inspired in some of its followers a mood of hatred and violence. It is our misfortune that part, though by no means all or even most, of the Muslim world is now going through such a period, and that much, though again not all, of that hatred is directed against us. **- Bernard Lewis**

BEHIND ALL THE FEARS of religious extremism, creeping sharia law and sleeper-cell terrorism lies the spectre of the angry Muslim. It is not hard to imagine that the faces behind the veils are scowling at the world around them, its decadence and faithlessness, and hoping for something better. After all, extremists protesting cartoons of the Prophet Mohammed or suicide bombers' final video messages express a total and uncontrollable rage at Western secular society. Does this rage spring from a general anger held by large numbers of Muslim immigrants? Is there a wellspring of bitterness and disenchantment that will yield even more violence and extremism?

Actually, Muslims appear to be among the least disenchanted and most satisfied people in the West. We already saw that Muslim immigrants are unusually content with their host countries, governments and democratic institutions. Recent years have seen a series of major investigations into the broader feelings and beliefs of these Muslims, and the results are both unambiguous and reassuring.

British Muslims, according to Gallup, are half as likely as average Britons to have experienced feelings of anger the previous day, and slightly less likely than ordinary Britons to report "experiencing a lot of negative emotions, including anger." They are about as likely as ordinary Britons (76% for Muslims and 82% for the general public) to report "feeling a lot of enjoyment." French Muslims are even less angry than the Brits. They are more likely than the French population to say they feel well rested or that they "smiled and laughed a lot" the day before the survey. Only 19% of French Muslims said they "felt a lot of anger the day before the survey," versus 33% of French people in general. They were equally likely to report feeling a lot of enjoyment.[72]

Two French academics conducted detailed surveys that found that Muslim immigrants in France were more likely to "have feelings of closeness with other French people" (85%) than they did with members of their own religious group (71%) or people of the same national origin (77%)—that is, Muslims felt slightly more comfortable in the company of non-Muslim French people than they did with other Muslims. Interestingly, this doesn't appear to be a product of secularization. Among self-declared Muslims—that is, those who define themselves by their religion rather than their nationality—the feeling of "closeness with other French people" was even higher, at 90%. It should be noted that only 84% of non-Muslim French people felt "feelings of closeness" with other French people.[73]

In the United States, where recent incidents of Islamic terrorism have led to fears of a wider disenchantment within the Muslim community, the results are also dramatic. Muslims in America are more likely to say they are "satisfied with their lives" (84% for foreign-born Muslims) than average Americans are (75%). Not only that, but that satisfaction rises to 90% for second-generation Muslims, born in the United States to immigrant parents. About the same number of Muslims (79%) as ordinary Americans (83%) say that their community is an "excellent" or "good" place to live. Even among Muslims living in neighbourhoods whose community mosque has been vandalized, fully 76% reported that their community is a good place.[74]

Obviously, there are *some* Muslims who are very angry. Some individual immigrants and their children in the West have become enraged enough to take up acts of violent revenge. But we can see from these studies that their acts don't spring from a wider anger in the general Muslim community. Still, even if Muslim immigrants are not harbouring rage at the world around them, is it possible that some of them are finding joy in the violent spectacles of jihad?

CLAIM:

Significant numbers of Muslims cheer for terrorist violence.

Clearly the Islamic jihad being waged today by Osama bin Laden and his compatriots all over the globe has great appeal among Muslims, and as bin Laden and other jihadists consistently portray themselves as the pure Muslims who are practicing the true Islam, it is clear that that portrayal is convincing to all too many. **- Robert Spencer**

Many European Muslims may themselves be moderates, yet may have a concept of religious identity that makes it difficult for them to side with infidels against even the most violent of their fellow Muslims . . .
- Bruce Bawer

WHEN A TERRORIST ATTACK occurs in the West, it's sometimes hard to avoid wondering if our Muslim neighbours might be watching in silent approval. It doesn't make sense for them to do so, given that 88% of the victims of Islamic terrorism are Muslim,[75] but after the violence of the last decade it can be hard not to wonder what side they're really on.

It is chilling to learn that 7% of American Muslims say that acts of violence against civilian targets, such as bombings, are "sometimes justified" if the cause is right, and that an additional 1% say they are "often justified."[76] This represents tens of thousands of people, after all. Taken in isolation, such poll results have become fodder for a widespread belief that ordinary Muslims condone terrorist violence. But those numbers leave out the larger context. When the same question was asked of Americans in general, an astounding 24% said they believe that bomb attacks aimed at civilians are "often or sometimes justified" and 6% feel they are "completely justified."[77] In other words, American Muslims are between four and six times *less likely* than other Americans to endorse violent acts against civilians. Of course, most citizens will interpret this question as referring to the acts of their nation's military in a declared war, but so will supporters of jihadi terrorism, who tend to view it as a legitimate war against infidel presence in the lands of Islam.

There are obviously Muslims who support terrorist violence enough to commit it themselves, sometimes within their own country. The question is whether they are a handful of lone actors whose views are alien to the people around them or if they are carrying out acts that are an extension of, and have the broad support of, views held by sections of the wider Muslim community.

The facts are unambiguous here. Across the Western world, support for violence and terrorism among Muslims is no higher than that of the general population, and in some cases it is lower. When a large-scale survey asked if "attacks on civilians are morally justified," 1% of the French public, 1% of the German public and 3% of the British public answered yes; among Muslims in the capital cities of those countries, the responses were a statistically indistinguishable 2%, 0.5%, and 2%. Asked if it is "justifiable to use violence for a noble cause," 7% of the French public agreed, along with 8% of French Muslims; 10% of the German public and fewer than 2% of German Muslims; 10% of the British public and 8% of British Muslims. The majority who said it was "not justifiable" was usually somewhat higher among Muslims than among non-Muslims.[78]

During the peak years of the Iraq War, a number of individual surveys showed higher levels of Muslim-immigrant anger at the United States, Britain and other Western governments participating in the war, and a degree of sympathy for al Qaeda. In 2007, for example, only 63% of foreign-born Muslims in the United States had "very unfavourable" views of al Qaeda. But that appears to have been a passing moment. By 2010, it had risen 12 percentage points to 75%, not far from the disapproval levels of the general public. Actual outright admiration of al Qaeda was very low (though still disturbing): 3% of American Muslims had a "somewhat favourable" view of al Qaeda and 2% had a "very favourable" view. Given that those numbers are higher than the numbers of Muslims who show strong support for violence against civilians, it's reasonable to conclude that much of this support is not for al Qaeda's terrorist attacks, but for the group's renegade image and political message, which by then had become a generic anticapitalist, anti-imperialist narrative not that different from more popular left-wing and anti-globalization voices.[79]

Most people understand that terrorism, or the leaders who endorse it, will never have more than a tiny minority of support in any community, whatever its motives. But much more widely held is the belief that a great many Muslims are seeking to impose their religious laws on their host countries, a view that has come to consume Western politics.

CLAIM:

Muslims want to set up "sharia courts" in Western countries.

Muslims promoting sharia believe that Islamic law must supersede the law of the land because sharia is divinely ordained and recognizes no superior secular authority. That alone should be reason enough to oppose the operation of sharia courts. For if the law of the land is not recognised by a section of the population, society will at best fragment into areas of separate development and at worst eventually adopt Islamic values overall. **- Melanie Phillips**

Once the door is open, the sky's the limit. The whole premise of sharia, after all, is that it applies to everything in life—not just food and domestic quarrels. The notion of separating the state from religion is utterly alien to the spirit and the letter of sharia, which . . . prescribes the death penalty for apostates, homosexuals, and adulteresses—and that's just for starters. **- Bruce Bawer**

THERE IS AN ELEMENT of truth in this claim. While there has never been an actual court in the West that has followed the Koranic religious codes known as sharia law, during the 1990s and the first decade of the twenty-first century there were several initiatives in Western countries, some of them successful, to create Islamic tribunals that could be used by believers to settle disputes and marriage issues among themselves according to religious law. These voluntary tribunals, modelled after existing religious panels used by Orthodox Jews and Roman Catholics, have been extremely controversial, and there are some good reasons to be concerned about them—though not the reasons usually given by the Muslim-tide activists.

In the 1980s and '90s some Western governments (mainly in English-speaking countries) moved to promote the use of alternative dispute resolution—a system in which citizens contesting contracts, divorces and other torts are encouraged to settle their differences among themselves, with the help of an independent mediator from the community, rather than embarking on a costly civil trial or lawsuit. For governments, such an approach helped reduce the case-load in civil courts and the soaring public cost of the justice system; for potential litigants or couples seeking a divorce, an inheritance deci-sion or a child-custody settlement, it often produced a satisfactory resolution without the hostility, complexity and cost of a court case.

It wasn't long before religious leaders, who have been ruling on such matters for centuries and who often prize their own scriptural laws above those of civil society, began seeking a place in this system. In the early 1990s, Jewish and Catholic tribunals were created under these laws in Britain, Canada and the United States. Their activities escaped the notice of the general public, though some legal observ-ers expressed alarm that the tribunals were giving official legitimacy to spiritual decisions that clashed with the values of a secular society. The Jewish tribunals, known within the faith as Beth Din, recognize a form of religious divorce known as a get, in which the husband hands the wife a document written in Aramaic and ancient Hebrew declaring the marriage over.

It was inevitable that religious Muslims would want to join Christians and Jews in offering arbitration services. Their first and most explosive attempt was in the Canadian province of Ontario. The province's Arbitration Act of 1991 authorized family-based tri-bunals run by Catholic and Jewish religious authorities to settle issues of divorce, inheritance or custody, as long as they didn't conflict with Canadian law. In 2003, Muslim organizations asked to have the act extended to include their faith, and proposed an Islamic Institute of Civil Justice to perform arbitrations. The province, unsettled by loud protests coming from conservatives, Christian activists and some secular Muslims, asked the former attorney-general Marion Boyd to investigate. Her 2004 report suggested that the government authorize the Muslim tribunals, partly because it might be unconstitutional to allow only Christians and Jews to have such tribunals. The protests intensified and attracted international media attention.

After a heated year of debate, Ontario premier Dalton McGuinty announced in September 2005 that "there will be no sharia law in Canada," and drew a sharp line between church and state by stripping all faith-based arbitrations of their legal authority, ending the 14-year experiment in state-recognized religious law. Almost immediately, Catholic and Jewish organizations joined forces with Muslim groups to begin lobbying to restore faith-based arbitration, but there has been little appetite among Canadian governments for a return.

Britain continues to allow Islamic dispute-settlement tribunals, known as Sharia Councils. They began in the 1980s, organized by conservative Deobandi Muslims for use within their community. The councils became recognized by the UK government in 1996, when the Arbitration Act allowed Christian, Jewish and Muslim tribunals to make rulings on civil matters; if both parties have voluntarily agreed to the arbitration, then their rulings are considered legally binding. In 2007, the more liberal Barelvi Muslims established a competing body, the Muslim Arbitration Tribunals. From the perspective of some Muslims, these tribunals solved a problem faced by immigrant women who had earlier married a Pakistani man under Pakistan's sharia-based laws: a British divorce does not provide them with the religious certificate that allows them to marry again. These religious divorces (which sometimes accompany a civil divorce conducted under British law) account for the majority of the tribunals' activity.

Britain's sharia tribunals have attracted considerable protest, not just from Eurabia writers but also from civil libertarians who worry that they are giving official recognition to discriminatory practices. For example, when dividing up the estate of a dead father, under sharia law the daughters are given half as much as the sons. The council also adjudicates the talaq, an Islamic divorce where, as with the Jewish get, the husband simply renounces his wife. It, too, is not available to women.

Much of the outrage over "stealth sharia" in the United States concerns such tribunals. They have existed within US mosques and Muslim communities for decades, and are considered a legitimate form of conflict mediation, and therefore are considered binding, under the Federal Arbitration Act of 1925 (which does not specifically mention religious tribunals). But there is a difference. The strict separation of church and state provided by the First Amendment means that US courts cannot review, consider, or hear appeals of decisions arising from religious tribunals. There has been some debate about whether courts can review decisions related to entirely non-religious matters adjudicated by the tribunals, such as division of property, but as a study in the *Columbia Law Review* concluded, "religious issues permeate the entirety of religious tribunal proceedings," so that the recognition of any of their decisions as legally binding would likely conflict with the First Amendment.[80]

So the problem of "sharia courts" is not really one of Muslims trying to impose their religious laws on their new homeland—no serious Muslim figure has suggested that—but the far more thorny question of whether religious believers (of any faith) should be allowed to make decisions based on their beliefs rather than on the laws of their country. From that perspective, one of the more beneficial outcomes of the Muslim-tide hysteria is that public anger over Islamic tribunals could draw attention to the larger problem of religious incursion into public life, resulting in a wider move toward secularization.

This is certainly what happened in Ontario. Something similar happened in France, where political outcry over Islam caused the government to ban from school classrooms not only the Muslim headscarf but also the Jewish yarmulke and the Christian cross. So, paradoxically enough, the rise of Islam in the West could prove to be a triumph for secularism.

But some argue that banishing religious tribunals will lead some religious Muslims, Orthodox Jews and Catholics to continue them in private, producing outcomes that promote inequality and discrimination. This has long been a dilemma in countries with constitutionally protected state secularism, including Turkey, France and the United States. Sometimes they conclude that the best approach is to place religious power within the fold of the legal system. A cornerstone of Turkey's constitutional secularism is that all 60,000 Turkish imams are government employees, paid and regulated by the Ministry of Religious Affairs, which even specifies the texts they may read in their sermons. This, Turks argue, is why Islamic extremism and terrorism have been almost nonexistent in their country: the fundamentalist religious movements financed by Saudi Arabia and Egypt have never been able to gain a foothold by paying the salaries of imams, as those countries do in the West.

Some Western governments have begun to adopt this approach. A number of European countries, notably Belgium, have begun paying the salaries of some imams, and others, including France and Germany, have set up publicly funded training and certification courses for imams in university religious studies departments and divinity schools. Two results, both potentially beneficial, could come from such policies. They could replace foreign-salaried extremist religious leaders with a generation of culturally integrated, linguistically fluent imams who advance the cause of moderation and modernity in the mosques of Europe. Or they could provoke a backlash that would put an end to all government involvement in religion, Ontario-style, and advance the cause of secularism.

However governments choose to respond to these sharia tribunals—by enforcing a strict secularism or by tolerating some forms of voluntary arbitration among religious believers—it is clear they are confronting not a general assault upon our legal system by Islam but a private matter among circles of religious believers that need not have any effect on the wider world. Whether Muslims believe that their religious laws should become the official laws of the countries around them is another question entirely.

CLAIM:

Muslim immigrants are pushing for sharia law in the West.

The Muslim immigrants do not want to integrate into a modern, tolerant state and they want to impose Sha'ria law on us all. **- Bat Ye'or**

Stealth jihadis use political, cultural, societal, religious, intellectual tools; violent jihadis use violence. But in fact they're both engaged in jihad, and they're both seeking to impose the same end state, which is to replace Western civilization with a radical imposition of Sharia.
- Newt Gingrich

To put it briefly and nakedly, the West is on the road to sharia.
- Bruce Bawer

THE PROPHET KNOWN AS Moses in Judaism and Christianity, and as Musa in Islam, received tablets printed with ten commandments from his god, according to the holy books of all three religions. Those commandments form the basis of Jewish Halacha and Talmudic law, Christian divine and Biblical law, and Islamic sharia law. The religious laws differ little in substance between the three faiths, but their interpretations do. The death penalty for those who convert, contained in the Torah and the Koran, has rarely been practised by Jews in recent centuries, but can still be found in the legal codes of some Muslim countries. It is held to be necessary among the most fanatical believers, leading to outbreaks of such practices as honour killing and the stoning of adulterers in parts of

Afghanistan, Yemen and Nigeria. Islam also has a number of cultural traditions, such as covering the heads of women, which have little support in the Koran (this is actually an Arabic tradition that pre-dates Islam) but are often mistakenly thought to be part of sharia, including by some believers.

As a result, it is hard to know what some Muslims mean when they say they favour sharia law. Do they simply mean that murder and theft should be illegal, and the law given a holy imprimatur? Or do they mean to follow the most extreme punishments of Islamic law, including cutting off a hand for theft, stoning for adultery, whipping for alcohol consumption and death for homosexuality, apostasy or conversion?

Likewise, when we learn that a majority of Christians in the United States say that they want laws to be based on the Ten Commandments, do they mean that conversion to another religion should be punished as a crime as serious as murder (as the First Commandment suggests) or that pictures of God or Jesus Christ should be forbidden (as the Second Commandment says, and some Protestants believe)? A few probably do, but the vast majority have something much milder in mind, probably not terribly different from existing US law.

Even in Muslim countries, sharia varies widely in popularity. In Indonesia, home to the world's largest population of Muslims, only 14% believe that laws should be based solely on sharia. In Iran, only 12% of men and 14% of women do—perhaps a response to the rather harsh and uncompromising interpretation of sharia imposed by the country's clerical dictatorship. On the other hand, half of Jordanians, strong majorities of Pakistanis and Afghans, and 70% of Egyptian men prefer sharia-based law (those countries already have legal systems based at least partly on sharia).

It's worth comparing these attitudes toward religious law with those in Western countries. Gallup found that the majority of

Americans want legislation to be drawn from the Bible: 46% said scripture should be "a source" of laws, and an additional 9% said it should be "the only source" of law. Likewise, 42% of Americans "want religious leaders to have a direct role in writing a constitution"—something that would probably be forbidden by the Constitution—and 55% want them to play no role. Interestingly, Iranians gave exactly the same response to that question.[81] Outside of the United States, far fewer Westerners support the idea of scriptural law—but the American example shows that this is not strictly an East-West divide. A certain proportion of every religious population will consist of antinomians—people who believe that the laws of God are superior to those of man.

When Muslims move to the West, their interest in religious-based law declines. Muslims in the United States, despite the public outcry over "stealth sharia," seem overwhelmingly uninterested in having Koranic law applied to themselves, to say nothing of Americans at large. A study of Muslim-American attitudes to sharia conducted by a Canadian law professor in 2012 interviewed a representative sample of Muslim religious and legal figures across the United States. "None of the 212 respondents—including many imams, legal scholars, Muslim lawyers and others working in the legal system—suggested that the courts should directly apply Islamic law to Muslims (or non-Muslims). Just three imams (of 41) proposed the creation of a parallel Islamic family tribunal, with the vast majority rejecting this idea in favor of recourse to the civil courts. Many Muslims see the civil courts as 'man's law,' in contrast with sharia which is 'god's law,' but are equally clear that they are required to obey the law of the land—this was emphasized over and over again—and see no incompatibility."[82]

A large poll of French Muslims conducted by *Le Monde* in 2008 found that 75% were "opposed to the imposition" of sharia, while

37% said "some elements of sharia could be applied if they were adapted to French law." And 17% felt that sharia should have jurisdiction in all countries.

British Muslims, according to a poll taken by the think tank Policy Exchange in 2007, held similar broad opinions. Asked "If I could choose, I would prefer to live in Britain under sharia law rather than British law," 75% of Muslims over the age of 45 preferred British law, a number that declined to 63% for 35- to 44-year-olds and just more than half for those under 35.[83]

In other words, an alarmingly large number of people feel that religion should trump secular law, though they are still a minority within a minority. But these figures do not tell us what we really want to know: How many Muslims in the West support the harsher interpretations of sharia, the stonings and executions and honour killings? To understand that, we need to ask some more specific questions. As mentioned above, in many countries—with some exceptions such as Britain—Muslim immigrants and especially their offspring are adopting the ideas of gender equality and tolerance of sexual minorities that have become widespread in the West.

A survey of three European countries on capital punishment—central to the nastier interpretations of sharia—found that 35% of all French people, 27% of Germans and 50% of Britons felt that the death penalty is "morally acceptable," while only 24% of French Muslims, 27% of German Muslims, and fully 63% of British Muslims believe it is. On the question of honour killings, the figures for the French, German and British general public who approve (2%, 1%, 1%) are similar enough to those of Muslims in those countries (3%, 3%, 2%) to fall within the survey's margin of error, and suggest that the practice has negligible support. In other words, the occasional disturbing instances of honour-killing murder in these countries are not tied to a broader Muslim acceptance of the practice.[84]

These findings suggest that Muslims in the West are far less interested in religious commandments than Muslims in the countries from
which they immigrated, but that like earlier religious-minority immigrants, they remain more faith-driven than the rest of the population.
If you consider their strong expressions of loyalty to their host countries and their institutions, as well as their low tolerance for violence,
Muslims' views about religion and law are little different from those
of, for example, Christians in the United States. The figures do point to
a portion of the population in Europe who, like earlier waves of poor
immigrants, are having an awkward and difficult period of integration.
In some instances (such as in Britain), they are clinging to traditional
social views, despite the rapid trend of secularization across most of
the Muslim world. But this does not suggest that there is any widespread desire or drive to make sharia law a reality in the West. Those
who support sharia appear to be the Muslims who are most marginal
and disconnected from society. Those with the best chance of influenc-
ing the legal system are those who are least interested in religious law.

"To put it in perspective," the American researchers Wajahat Ali
and Matthew Duss write, "the extreme Christian right in America has
been trying for decades to inscribe its view of America as a 'Christian
nation' into our laws. They have repeatedly failed in a country in
which more than three-quarters of people identify as Christians. It's
extremely unlikely that an extreme faction of American Muslims, a
faith community that constitutes approximately 1% of the U.S. population, would have more success."[85] If the West's secular, pluralist
institutions have any value at all, they should be able to incorporate
another minority of sincere religious believers, as they have done
with several in the past.

But even if the majority of Muslims support neither terrorism nor
religious law, it still seems possible that their religious beliefs are producing terrorism. If their beliefs are causing even a small minority of

Muslims to become terrorists, then how can we tolerate the larger community? To understand this concern, we need to look closely at the actual roots of terrorism.

CLAIM:

Terrorism is a natural and inevitable extension of fundamentalist Islamic faith.

It's not merely that there's a global jihad lurking within this religion, but that the religion itself is a political project—and, in fact, an imperial project—in a way that modern Christianity, Judaism, Hinduism, and Buddhism are not. Furthermore, this particular religion is historically a somewhat bloodthirsty faith in which whatever's your bag violence-wise can almost certainly be justified. **- Mark Steyn**

Apologists would tell us that militant Islam is a distortion of Islam, but that is not true; it emerges out of the religion, constituting a radically new interpretation. It adapts an age-old faith to the political requirements of our day. **- Daniel Pipes**

JIHADIST TERRORISTS ARE religious believers: that much is undeniable. They invoke Allah and the Koran, they denounce their targets for being unholy, they speak of a divine calling and a scriptural obligation to avenge the "crusader" and the "infidel." This leads to a widespread belief that al Qaeda and its offspring must be religious movements—which carries the frightening implication that any devout Muslim could potentially become a jihadist. Therefore, if a large percentage of Muslims are literalist believers, and they all are required to embrace the same violent and vengeful passages in the Koran with equal intensity, what is to stop any of your devout Muslim neighbours from strapping on an explosive belt? This logic has led to one of the core ideas behind the popularity of the Muslim-tide movement: the idea that Muslims are all at least tangentially party to a war of conquest, and that the devout and the violent are part of the same larger cause.

This, however, is one area where a decade of counterterrorism research, the analysis of volumes of extremist literature and dialogue, and interviews with thousands of current and former jihadists and terror-cell members by large groups of scholars have produced two unambiguous conclusions. First, it is not generally devout or fundamentalist Muslims who become terrorists. Second, terrorists are driven by political belief, not by religious faith. The Muslims who support violence and terrorism are not the Muslims who are the most religious or fundamentalist in their views; in fact, the two rarely have anything to do with one another, and the latter are usually opposed to the former.

Perhaps the most detailed and comprehensive profile of Islamic recruits to terrorism was conducted in 2008 by the British intelligence agency MI5, whose behavioural science unit performed in-depth case studies on "several hundred individuals known to be involved in, or closely associated with, violent extremist activity," including jihadist fundraisers and would-be suicide bombers. The conclusion is that Muslim terrorists in the West "are a diverse collection of individuals, fitting no single demographic profile, nor do they all follow a typical pathway to violent extremism." As in other countries, they tend to be either converts or second-generation, native-born children of legal immigrants.

Significantly, extremist Muslim clerics generally have no role in the indoctrination or recruitment of these jihadists. "Far from being

Islamist fundamentalists," the report concludes, "most are religious novices." Very few have been raised in strongly religious households; in fact, MI5 concludes, "there is evidence that a well-established religious identity actually protects against violent radicalization."

Some recruits, the agency notes, "are involved in drug-taking, drinking alcohol and visiting prostitutes." But they don't appear to be mentally unstable, lone-wolf characters; in fact, a majority of those over 30 have steady relationships, and most have children. They also tend to be well educated and employed, albeit typically in low-income jobs. Rather than intense monastic religious devotees, they tend to be non-faithful individuals who are drawn to radical peer groups for political or personal, but not religious, reasons. The study concluded that four factors were leading to terrorist radicalization: "trauma," such as the death of a loved one (10% of terror suspects had experienced this); immigration without family members (a third of extremists had "migrated to Britain alone" as students or labourers); "criminal activity" (two-thirds had criminal records); and "prison" (many were radicalized while serving time).[86]

Indeed, religious devotion simply does not correlate with violent radicalism. In one study, the Gallup organization examined the 7% of Muslims worldwide who are considered "radical"—that is, who condone the September 11 attacks and view the United States unfavourably—and found that they are no more religious than the general population of Muslims.[87] Pew, in 2008, found that the proportion of non-religious German Muslims who said that "attacks on civilians cannot be morally justified" (94%) was identical to that of religious believers who said the same (94%). In France, it was 94% of religious French Muslims and 82% of the nonreligious; 90% of religious British Muslims and 87% of the nonreligious disapproved of attacks on civilians.[88]

Jihadist terrorism became a phenomenon in the West starting in the early 1990s as an extreme political response to the presence of Western soldiers in Islamic lands. It has continued to follow this political path. While this means that adherents must believe in the existence of an inviolate "land of Islam," it does not mean that they are otherwise the most devout religious believers.

"Religious orthodoxy and political radicalization are very different things and respond to very different mechanisms," says Rik Coolsaet, the Belgian scholar who has led some of the most detailed studies of Muslim radicalization. "Religious orthodoxy starts from a quest for identity, especially demanding in highly uncertain times. Political radicalization starts from opposition to injustice. The former can develop into a challenge for social cohesion if it leads individuals and groups into a cultural ghetto. The latter can eventually become a security threat if some individuals move further down the path to extremism that—for an even smaller number—eventually ends up in using violence as their preferred tool of political action."

Researchers at Demos spent two years studying Islamic religious radicals and convicted terrorists in Britain and Canada, and found that radical religious believers and terrorists were very distinct and different people. "[Religious] radicals also felt genuine affection for Western values of tolerance and pluralism, system of government, and culture. Terrorists, on the other hand, were unique in their loathing of Western society and culture. Interestingly, radicals were more likely than terrorists to have been involved in political protest, to have studied at university (and studied humanities or arts subjects) and to have been employed." The terrorists also "had a simpler, shallower conception of Islam than radicals—that is, their degree of interest in the actual teachings of the Koran was fairly minimal."[89]

Or, in the words of Olivier Roy, the French scholar of Islamic societies: "The process of violent radicalization has little to do with religious practice, while radical theology, as salafism, does not necessarily lead to violence." The radicalization process, Roy notes, "is not linked with the outspoken condemnation of Western sexual liberalisation that is pervasive among conservative Muslim circles . . . AQ [al Qaeda] recruits are not specifically puritanical and often live or have lived the usual life of western teenagers."[90]

Mark Fallon, a former US counterintelligence officer who heads the International Association of Chiefs of Police and oversaw the prosecution of dozens of high-level terror suspects, conducted a study of hundreds of ex-terrorists and found that neither theology nor larger political ideology played significant roles. "The one thing that we found everywhere is that the trigger that turns someone to violence is a very personal one and is usually based on local conditions. The global environment is used to recruit these people, but it's generally some local condition or individual event in that person's life that turns them. It wasn't about ideology; it wasn't about theology; it was about identity."[91] Of course, people who join terrorist cells, however political or personal their motives, have become religious believers, and most of them hold broadly fundamentalist or Salafist views of the world, however vague. In some cases they are recruited into jihadist organizations through evangelical Islamic movements such as Tablighi Jamaat, which are not themselves violent but are used by jihadist organizations seeking eager and vulnerable recruits. While this means that these religious orders should be watched closely, it does not follow that terrorism is a product of their religious doctrines.

Indeed, fundamentalists and religious Islamists are often the most effective forces among Muslim immigrants in *opposing* terrorist movements. In Britain, London's Metropolitan Police successfully purged the Finsbury Park mosque of al Qaeda–linked sympathizers and activists by working closely with Salafist groups prevalent in the community. Scotland Yard found that the Salafists (who seek a theocratic Muslim state through political means) had both the most detailed knowledge of fellow immigrants who were susceptible to terrorist radicalization and also the strongest determination to keep violent and jihadist tendencies out of their mosque. This was a controversial approach, as it involved working intimately with religious extremists whose social views were abhorrent and whose ultraconservative views of women and homosexuality were being battled by other sections of the Muslim community. But from what I witnessed, it did appear to be effective in ending the violent extremist influence on the neighbourhood.[92] Still, if terrorism is not a natural outgrowth of extreme Muslim religious beliefs, even those held by fundamentalists, couldn't it be a product of the dense clusters of poor, segregated Muslim immigrants in our cities? That, too, is a much-examined question.

CLAIM:

The growth of Muslim populations is accompanied by a growth in Islamic extremism and terrorism.

The jihad is coming quietly to America by the intentional building of Muslim populations in small to medium American cities.
- Pamela Gellar

What is the societal benefit of bringing in throwbacks, some of whom are no doubt terrorists, and some of whom are gonna produce children who will become terrorists? **- Michael Savage**

ISLAMIST TERRORISM IN the West has generally been declining. In Europe, the number of people charged for Islamist terrorism offences dropped from 201 in 2007 to 187 in 2008 to 110 in

2009. It then rose slightly to 179 in 2010, largely as a result of a sweep of arrests in France related to a cell of North Africans preparing to fight in Afghanistan, but this does not appear to be part of an upward trend.[93]

In the United States, there has been a false perception that Islamic terrorism is on the rise, in large part because of three high-profile incidents. These incidents were unrelated to one another but occurred in quick succession: the November 2009 Fort Hood shooting, in which a lone gunman killed 13 people on a military base; the December 2009 "underwear bomber" case (committed by a wealthy Nigerian man travelling to the United States); and the unsuccessful May 2010 Times Square bomb plot, committed by a lone Pakistani American with apparent ties to the Pakistani Taliban. But Islamist terrorism remains rare: the number of Muslim-American terrorism suspects and perpetrators apprehended each year averaged around 14 annually between 2001 and 2008*— then spiked to 47 in 2009, in large part because a group of 17 Somali Americans were arrested for joining the al-Shabaab militia in Somalia. Some observers, looking at this figure, together with the headlined attacks of 2009 and 2010, feared that it meant jihadism was on the increase. But then the number of terror arrests fell back to 26 in 2010,[94] and to 20 in 2011.[95] There does not appear to be a larger movement.

In the West, jihadist attacks are not as prevalent as other forms of terrorism. For example, 2010 saw 20 non-Islamic terror attacks in the United States (most of them right-wing). In Europe, there were three Islamist attacks with one casualty that year (all in Scandinavia) while there were 160 separatist attacks, 45 left-wing and anarchist

---

* The actual tally is probably lower because these numbers include acts of terrorism such as the 2003 Beltway sniper case that have no apparent Islamist or jihadist motives, but happen to have been committed by Muslims.

attacks, and 41 other attacks (mainly about a single issue). All told, there were 65 jihadist terrorist incidents in Europe from 2001 to 2009, involving 336 people; this represents less than 1% of all terrorist incidents on the continent during those years. None of this detracts from the seriousness of the Islamic terrorist threat, or the importance of countering radical ideologies in immigrant communities. Terrorism remains a grave problem, and has the potential to threaten international security. But it is not becoming epidemic, nor is it rising with the Muslim populations in the West.

The more important question is whether clusters of Muslim immigrants and their offspring—especially those who are living in high-density, ethnically segregated, poverty-stricken urban neighbourhoods—are becoming breeding grounds for anti-Western violence. By tolerating Muslim immigration, are the countries of the West welcoming more terrorists into their midst?

In short, this doesn't appear to be the case. High concentrations of Muslims are not generally a source of terrorism. Geographers Nissa Finney and Ludi Simpson analyzed the addresses of all British Muslims charged with terrorism offences in the mid-2000s decade, around the time of the London Underground bombings, and found that 77% of them came from neighbourhoods where less than 11% of the population was Muslim and more than half (56%) came from neighbourhoods with less than 6% Muslims; the lone Muslim living in a largely white neighbourhood is a closer fit to the terrorist profile.[96] A similar effect was found in the United States, where only 17% of terrorism suspects between 2001 and 2011 were found to be residents of high-concentration Muslim neighborhoods such as Dearborn and Los Angeles. The majority were from lone Muslim families in mixed neighbourhoods.[97] The former CIA counterterrorism specialist Marc Sageman, in his classic study of terrorist recruitment, found that the great majority of terrorists were neither poor and isolated nor from broken homes or criminal backgrounds: "Three quarters of my sample came from the upper or middle class. The vast majority—90%—came from caring, intact families. Sixty-three percent had gone to college, as compared with the 5 to 6 percent that's usual for the third world. These are the best and brightest young people of their societies in many ways."[98]

This result was confirmed in Britain by the MI5 report, which found that two-thirds of the terror suspects the spy organization had watched during the decade were "from middle or upper-middle-class backgrounds, showing that there is no simplistic relationship between poverty and involvement in Islamist extremism."[99] A 2011 Whitehall report found that 45% of English terror suspects had attended university, college or some other form of postsecondary education, a far higher proportion than the general English or Muslim population—and a strong indication that the poor Muslim neighbourhoods are not breeding grounds of terrorism. These suspects had come to their political convictions based on reading, Internet communication and contact with other political radicals in universities and prisons, not by way of influence from existing bodies of thought within Muslim communities or districts.

The image of the self-ghettoized Muslim living in a parallel society dissolves once you encounter the actual terrorists. When Edwin Bakker at the International Centre for Counter-Terrorism at The Hague scrutinized the data on hundreds of Muslim Europeans convicted of terrorism, he found that almost all were the European-born children or grandchildren of immigrants, and 305 out of the 313 suspects he identified were legal residents of a European country. Only eight had ever lived in a country outside Europe. Less than a fifth were raised in religious Muslim households; almost half had largely secular upbringings; and more than a third were converts to Islam, mainly from Christian backgrounds.

The convicted terrorists were reasonably well educated: 70% had finished secondary school, and the rest had graduated from college or university; there were no dropouts or illiterates. Of the 93 for whom economic data were available, 5 were upper class, 36 middle class and 52 were lower class; another 14 were entrepreneurs such as shopkeepers. Two-thirds were employed at the time of their arrest, the largest group in unskilled labour. While their ages ranged from 16 to 62, they were typically in their mid- to late twenties. Almost half were married, engaged or divorced, most of them with children; a fifth were single. Significantly, almost a fifth of them had already been convicted in a court for a non-terrorist offence.[100]

A number of major studies of the demographics and psychology of terrorist recruits have shown that adversity, including poverty and violence, is rarely a significant factor in radicalization or terrorist recruitment. If anything, it is the opposite, as middle-class, well-educated Muslims are drawn into jihad. These individuals are more likely to *perceive* a sense of shame or humiliation, and to have hopes and aspirations that they come to believe have been thwarted by the same Western forces they believe are invading the lands of Islam—as well as a desire for self-glorification that can be accomplished through martyrdom.[101]

"Clearly, absolute material conditions do not account for terrorism; otherwise, acts of terrorism would be committed more by the poorest individuals living in the poorest regions, and this is not the case," a major study of the psychology of terrorist recruitment concludes. "Psychological research points to the fundamental importance of *perceived* deprivation. . . . This groundswell of frustration and anger has given rise to greater sympathy for extremist 'antiestablishment' tactics among the vast populations on the ground floor."[102] People suffering *actual* deprivation do not have the time or inclination for terrorist organizing. Many of the most famous jihadists, including Mohamed Atta and Osama bin Laden, were university-educated technicians and engineers.

"All of them are integrated, Westernized and educated," Olivier Roy says of the Western terrorists. "They do not have any particular social background that would explain their political radicalization because of poverty or exclusion. Most of all, almost all of them become 'born again' in the West. . . . The source of radicalization is the West and not the jihad or the conflicts in the Middle East. None became a radical after attending religious studies completed in a Muslim-majority country. Finally, for almost each one of them, the time between their return to religion and their transit to political radicalization has been very short, which shows that they are as much, if not more so, interested in politics as in religion."[103]

Has Islamic terrorism been a natural outgrowth of the conservative religious and political beliefs of the immigrants and their children? Or has it been something more like the wave of left-wing terrorism that swept across the United States and Europe in the 1960s and '70s, in which thousands of mainly middle-class young people joined a dangerous movement that saw itself in opposition to the culture around it and committed hundreds of bombings through organizations such as the Weather Underground in the United States and the Red Army Faction in Germany?

The Demos researchers, in their study of religious extremists and violent radicals, found that al Qaeda's appeal in Europe was neither its theology nor its larger ideology but rather its image of antiauthoritarian radicalism: "An increasingly important part of al Qaeda's appeal in the West is its dangerous, romantic and counter-cultural characteristics. . . . It is becoming a combination of toxic ideology and youthful radicalism, something inherently anti-establishment which some young people find appealing. . . . Al-Qaeda inspired terrorism in the West shares much in common with other counter-cultural, subversive groups of predominantly angry young men."[104]

Jihadist terrorism, Olivier Roy notes, "shares many factors with other forms of dissent, either political or behavioral." Most radicals have broken with their families; they don't mention traditions of Islam or fatwas, but rather act on an individual basis and outside the usual bonds of family, mosque and Islamic association. Modern Islamic terrorism is "an avatar of ultra-leftist radicalism—its targets are the same as the traditional targets of the ultra-left—US imperialism, symbols of globalization."

The sons of immigrants who turn to violent jihad are, ironically enough, driven by a world view that is exactly the same as that of the Muslim-tide activists. They believe that there are two irreconcilable civilizations, one trying to dominate the other by infiltration and aggression, and that they must fight to protect their traditions and values from the outsiders. This vision, from either perspective, is false and dangerous. Extremism remains a serious enough threat that we need to invest care and attention in combating its underlying philosophies and psychological causes. We now know that the terrorists' "civilizational" vision is not shared by other Muslim immigrants and their children, that it does not emerge from their ethnic neighbourhoods, and that it does not spring from their practice of religion, however strict.

What we are left to contemplate is a group of new immigrants, large but not the largest, who come from poor and religious backgrounds, who are settling into the social, political and reproductive patterns of their new homes, but whose progress is sometimes interrupted economically and educationally, and therefore socially, by institutions that deny them the same opportunities as their native-born neighbours. This may feel like an unprecedented phenomenon. But, as we shall see in the next chapter, it is far from unprecedented. We have been through all of this before.

THREE

WE'VE BEEN HERE BEFORE

IT IS THE NATURE of the human mind that we tend to compress and simplify events of the past, remembering the traumas and crises of recent history as having been more brief and simple than they really were. Similar events occurring in our own time seem more complex, more unpredictable and more difficult to resolve. Psychologists call this hindsight bias: things loom larger and seem more permanent when they are not yet over.

The arrival of millions of people from poor religious-minority backgrounds in Western countries was a traumatic, politically controversial, sometimes violent affair that occupied front pages and stood at the forefront of our political consciousness for the better part of two generations. We tend to remember earlier waves of southern European Catholics and Eastern European Jews as having arrived in rags, settled in colourful urban neighbourhoods and, in English-speaking countries at least, quickly found prosperity and melted into our populations. We forget that the sons of arrivals from Poland and Ireland failed to do better economically than their fathers, were often more religiously extreme, and refused to marry outside their ethnic circle. We forget that this was considered a threat to our democracy and civilization. We forget that it was nearly universal, for nearly three-quarters of a century, to see these people as members of an alien civilization, to distrust them because of the presumed motives of their religion, to associate them with violence, to believe that they were deliberately refusing to integrate—and that there was plenty of evidence to support such views. Indeed, the integration of Catholic and Jewish immigrants into our economies and societies took far longer than we remember. We cannot help but think that things are different this time. To avoid the mistakes of hindsight, we should take the time to remember.

I THE CATHOLIC TIDE

IF YOU LIVED IN the United States in 1949 and 1950, it would have been almost impossible to avoid Paul Blanshard's book *American Freedom and Catholic Power*. It spent 11 months on the *New York Times* bestseller list, received a recommendation from the Book-of-the-Month Club, sold 240,000 copies in its first edition and went through 26 printings in the US and internationally; a second edition, in 1958, was also a hit. While this book has all but vanished from the public imagination, for a while, it seemed as if the coffee table in every Anglo-American educated middle-class home held a copy.

The idea that seized the day? Blanshard was sounding the alarm over the flood of Roman Catholic immigrants to the United States, which he warned was a profound threat to democracy, equality and secular values. They came from countries that were almost all authoritarian, religiously fundamentalist and opposed to the rights of women and the practice of birth control. Catholics adhered to a changeless, unalterable, clerically preordained dogma that was not so much a faith as a political ideology: "a survival of medieval authoritarianism that has no rightful place in the democratic American environment." Blanshard charged that Catholics could not and would not be integrated; they were establishing parallel societies in American cities and plotting to impose their beliefs even more widely. Catholicism was at root an "undemocratic system of alien control." Fast-reproducing Catholic families were "outbreeding the non-Catholic elements in our population" and would eventually seek to gain control of the presidency and install divine law through a "Catholic plan for America" that would include a constitutional amendment making the United States a "Catholic republic."

He found evidence of the Catholic penchant for extreme social control in their black headscarf–wearing religious extremists: nuns. Nuns represented the Church's attempt, he wrote, to recreate "an age when women allegedly enjoyed subjection and reveled in self-abasement." Furthermore, he claimed that most criminals in American cities were Catholic, and that violence, fascism, crime and terrorism accompanied any large Catholic population. America required a "resistance movement" to oppose the "antidemocratic social policies of the hierarchy and . . . every intolerant or separatist or un-American feature of those policies."

Blanshard was far from being a fringe pamphleteer or a religious crank. He was a senior editor of the *Nation,* an activist lawyer and prosecutor appointed by New York's mayor, Fiorello La Guardia, to head the Department of Investigations and Accounts, where he uncovered graft and corruption. In earlier incarnations he had been a State Department official and a successful foreign correspondent. In short, Blanshard was a respected figure of American secular thought. Much like Bruce Bawer or Geert Wilders in a later generation, he was a committed liberal who saw in the conservatism of the new immigrant neighbourhoods a set of grave threats to the foundations of liberalism. Albert Einstein and Bertrand Russell praised his book, and John Dewey spoke of its "exemplary scholarship, good judgement, and tact."

And his book was far from being a lone work. As the historian John T. McGreevy recounts: "According to the editors at the *New Republic* and the *Nation,* a broad group of faculty members in the humanities and social sciences, and many influential figures in Reform Judaism and mainline Protestantism, Catholic authoritarianism might quash the scientific spirit, produce adults incapable of psychological autonomy, and have a disastrous effect on national unity because of the growing number of children enrolled in Catholic schools."[1] The

American theologian Reinhold Niebuhr issued warnings, as did the historian Lewis Mumford and Dewey, who believed that Catholics could become a fifth column.

Just as the Muslim-tide literature is an alarmist response to the genuine threat of jihadist terrorism and Islamist fundamentalism, Blanshard and his movement were reacting to the very real problems of fascism and backwardness across much of the Roman Catholic world, which often carried over into political extremism and mass criminality in Irish and Italian neighbourhoods. Catholic immigrants had been coming in great numbers for seven decades, and some of them seemed to be becoming less, not more, integrated. Terrorist attacks carried out in the United States and Britain by Irish and Italians were fresh in people's minds. Catholic groups were lobbying for separate religious education. The world had just been through the terrible shock of the war and the decades of totalitarianism, during which the Catholics of Spain, Italy and Austria had become outright fascists; their diasporas had seen explosions of extremism. As for Ireland, its loyalties in the war had been darkly ambiguous. Immigrants from any of these countries seemed to be carrying their spiritual and ideological diseases with them, ready to infect their new hosts.

This was also the prevalent view in postwar Canada, where vast labour shortages had produced a desperate need for immigration from beyond its traditional frontiers of Britain and northern Europe. Repeatedly, internal government memos warned that European Catholics could not be assimilated into democratic countries. The Italian, according to a memo from Laval Fortier, commissioner for overseas immigration, "is not the type we are looking for in Canada. His standard of living, his way of life, even his civilization seems so different that I doubt if he could even become an asset to our country." Italians, along with most other Catholic groups, were classed as "non-preferred." Nevertheless, large numbers arrived.[2]

Blanshard himself held up the example of Canada as a warning, citing Quebec's Catholic majority and provincial funding of separate Catholic school boards. "In Canada," he wrote, "the Roman Church has built a state within a state because the British government permitted public revenue to be used for a school system that conditioned Catholic children to be Catholics first and Canadians second. Many Canadians believe that it is too late now to rescue the province of Quebec from medieval forces and that, like Eire, it should become a separate nation."[3]

This postwar eruption of anti-Catholic fear was not the first time the prospect of a "Catholic tide" had inflamed the North American public. When large-scale immigration from the Catholic countries of Europe began in earnest in the late nineteenth century, the newcomers struck many citizens as members of a completely different civilization, who formed their own neighbourhoods and education systems, lobbied the government to allow them to live under their religious laws, and brought with them forms of violence—including nationalist and anarchist terrorism—that had not previously emerged from religious-minority communities. The Irish, the Italians, the Eastern European Jews: each in succession was seen as something different and unprecedented. Each time, the same line was heard: *Earlier waves of immigrants were from a race and civilization similar to ours, but this group is different: they come from an alien culture, and can never share our values.*

The boundaries of "our civilization," as defined by English-speaking people, kept changing. First it was limited to people from the British Isles (minus Ireland), then to northwestern Europe (after Germans and Scandinavians were accepted in the late nineteenth century); only in the late twentieth century was "our civilization" allowed to encompass all of Western Europe. As early as 1922, the scholar John Palmer Gavit recognized the pattern: "Each phase of immigration [to North America] has been 'the new immigration' at its time; each has been viewed with alarm; each has been described as certain to deteriorate the physical quality of our people and destroy the standard of living and citizenship."[4]

In the two decades following the Great Famine of the 1840s, hundreds of thousands of Irish had come to England, forming huge, largely segregated slums in London. While they were British subjects in the eyes of the law, in the eyes of most Londoners they were untrustworthy, strange foreigners. In 1867, Irish nationalists set off a bomb against the wall of Clerkenwell Prison in an effort to free imprisoned militants, killing six passersby. Suddenly Catholics were also potential terrorists. That bombing shocked London, and the city was soon filled with rumours of Irish terrorists digging tunnels beneath the Thames to blow up Big Ben and St. Paul's cathedral; a call for citizens to patrol the streets attracted 166,000 volunteers. Over the years that followed, Fenians would dynamite dozens of public locations including Scotland Yard, London Bridge, the House of Commons, the Tower of London, and several times in the 1880s, with devastating effect, the London Underground. Before these attacks, people had simply looked askance at their cloistered, deeply religious Irish neighbours; now they feared them.

As with the Islamist bombers today, the public tended to see Irish political violence not as a matter of politics or nationality but simply as an extension of the immigrants' religion. The Irish immigrants of the time, historian Leo Lucassen concluded, "were *generally* detested because they were poor and nationalistic, but *predominantly* so because they were Catholic. . . . Catholicism was perceived by the largely Anglican native population as representing an entirely different culture and worldview, and it was feared because of the faith's global and expansive aspirations."[5]

William Gladstone, between terms as Liberal prime minister, wrote an enormously popular pamphlet, *The Vatican Decrees*, which argued that Catholics in Britain could not be loyal both to the British state and to the Pope (whom the Vatican had declared infallible in 1870). Catholicism, he wrote, was not a spiritual faith but "an Asian monarchy: nothing but one giddy height of despotism, and one dead level of religious subservience." Catholics were determined to replace the liberties of Britain with authoritarianism, impose their "direct antagonism to the liberal tendencies of the age," and hide their "crimes against liberty beneath a suffocating cloud of incense." His pamphlet soon became a hit in the United States, too, where Catholic immigration, previously the target of roadside preachers, populist movements and assorted cranks, had suddenly become a grave concern of the country's elites.

America has, of course, always been a country of immigrants, but earlier waves had been overwhelmingly Protestant. The majority of Irish newcomers to that point had been Scots-Irish Protestants; they were joined by Germans and Nordic peoples, also Protestants and also gradually accepted. Starting in the 1880s, though, immigrants to North America were far greater in number, and increasingly from southern and eastern Europe. By 1896, and for decades afterwards, the majority of immigrants to America were Orthodox Christians, Jews, and very largely Roman Catholics. In 1882, only 13% of immigrants to the United States came from southern and eastern Europe; by 1907, that proportion had risen to 81%—and the annual flow of immigrants had doubled, from 648,000 to 1.2 million. By far the largest group were the Catholics. Italy alone contributed 200,000 immigrants a year throughout the century's first decade. By 1920, several of the founding states were approaching Catholic-majority status.

Francis Walker, the superintendent of the US Census Bureau, worried in 1896 that this new Catholic-dominated immigration "is a matter which no intelligent patriot can look upon without the gravest apprehension and alarm. They are beaten men from beaten races, representing the worst failures in the struggle for existence." Walker had become convinced that the high Catholic (and Jewish) birth rate was going to swamp the US population because native-born Americans had become too complacent and morally defeated to bring sufficiently large numbers of children into the world.[6]

The fast-reproducing Catholics and Jews were considered a grave threat, especially as native-born Americans appeared to allow a life of relative comfort and urbanization to lower their reproduction rates. Even President Theodore Roosevelt expressed alarm, instructing the native-born American woman to become "a good wife, a good mother, able and willing to perform the first and greatest duty of womanhood, to bring up as they should be brought up, healthy children, sound body, mind, and character, and numerous enough so that the race shall increase and not decrease." Huge numbers of Americans read the warning from anthropologist Madison Grant, in a dozen editions of his scientific-racist *Passing of the Great Race*, that "the rapid decline of the birth rate of native Americans because of the poorer classes of Colonial stock will not bring children into the world to compete in the labour market with the Slovak, the Italian, the Syrian and the Jew."

Among the most ardent opponents of Catholic immigration were the pioneering feminists and women's suffrage activists of the late nineteenth century. Foreshadowing the arguments of anti-Islamic feminists a century later, they warned that the strict and unchangeable sexual inequality of Catholic doctrine imprisoned women, and that Catholic immigration set back the cause of female equality. "It is not possible," wrote Elizabeth Cady Stanton, one of the founders of the American women's rights movement, "for a foreigner and a Catholic to take in the grandeur of the American idea of individual rights. . . . The human mind is ever oscillating between the extremes of authority and individualism, and if the former—the Catholic idea—finds lodgement in the minds of this people, we ring the death-knell of American liberties."[7]

The threat of Catholic-immigrant takeover and violence soon became a major theme in federal elections. Rutherford B. Hayes, the nineteenth president, catapulted himself into national politics with an Ohio gubernatorial campaign in which he blasted his Democratic opponents for passing laws that allowed Catholic priests to visit state prisons and asylums, the thin edge of a wedge, he insisted, of an assault on basic freedoms. James Garfield, his successor in the White House, did the same, describing Catholic immigration as an assault on "modern civilization."[8] Literary figures joined the campaign, led by Ralph Waldo Emerson. "It is the political character of the Roman Church," he wrote, "that makes it incompatible with our institutions & unwelcome here." The editors of the *New York Times*, the *Chicago Tribune*, *Harper's Weekly* and the *Nation* all issued stern warnings about the Catholic threat.

Even though the panic over Catholic immigration existed on both the left and the right, it was far from a unanimous sentiment. There was a backlash among politicians who remembered that their own families had been subject to similar anti-immigrant manias. When Grover Cleveland, the twenty-second (and twenty-fourth) president, was asked to sign a bill in the 1880s requiring English fluency among immigrants, he noted that "the time is quite within recent memory when the same thing was said of immigrants who, with their descendents now, are amongst our best citizens." Such pro-immigrant opinions had a resurgence in the early twentieth century, too. This was the era that produced the term "melting pot" and the concepts of multiethnic pluralism that would only become majority opinions after the 1960s. At times during this era, it seemed that tolerance was becoming widespread.

But these inclusive attitudes could not yet compete with fears of Catholic-immigrant political extremism and violence, which took on a new intensity when a naturalized immigrant from a Catholic family in Eastern Europe, the radical anarchist Leon Czolgosz, assassinated President William McKinley in 1901. The assassination coincided with a rise of radical terrorist attacks and riots, many of them carried out by Italian and Eastern European Catholics, that culminated in the string of anarchist terror bombings committed by Italian Catholics in the late 1910s. While the motives for this violence lay in labour struggles and political anger, and certainly not in religion, the public and political leaders saw it as a direct consequence of immigration from the despotic, violence-plagued countries of the Catholic world.

Catholics were also distrusted because they appeared to have a political agenda. Whether Catholic immigrants were German, Italian or Irish, they tended to vote as a bloc. This, wrote historian Ray Billington, "created the impression that the immigrants were all acting in accord with a general command and that that command came from the Catholic Church."[9] Many Catholics were themselves divided over whether they should integrate into the society around them or huddle together to protect their families from a sinful, threatening world. While large numbers of European Catholics in the late nineteenth century were adopting liberalism or Gallicanism—the belief that the customs of the immigrant's new home should trump Church doctrine—in the United States, there was a movement against such modernization. "For much of the nineteenth century," two Catholic historians observed, "Catholics in America were the unassimilated, sometimes violent 'religious other.' Often they did not speak English or attend public schools. Some of their religious women—nuns—wore distinctive clothing. Their religious practices and beliefs—from rosaries to transubstantiation—seemed to many

Americans superstitious nonsense. Most worrisome, Catholics seemed insufficiently grateful for their ability to build churches and worship in a democracy, rights sometimes denied to Protestants and Jews in Catholic countries, notably Italy."[10]

Father Bernard Hafkenscheid, America's leading Jesuit, warned his followers against assimilating too much by noting that "we are children of the Church and the truth; our adversaries are heretics or unbelievers; it is, then, our duty to take the offensive and to expose to the public the erroneous doctrines of Protestantism and impiety." As with future religious-minority populations, the second generation of Catholic immigrants often descended into forms of conservatism and fundamentalism that would have been alien in their home countries. It proved temporary (most Catholics are liberals now), but in those early waves it tended to confirm some of the worst stereotypes about Catholics.

In response to mounting public alarm, Washington spent an unprecedented sum on the Dillingham Commission into immigration. Its 41-volume report, published in 1911, noted that the United States was entirely a nation of immigrants, but divided the population neatly into offspring of "old immigration" (which, the report said, "was largely a movement of settlers who came from the most progressive sections of Europe for the purpose of making themselves homes in the New World") and "new immigration," much of it Catholic and Jewish (which was "largely a movement of unskilled labouring men who have come, in large part temporarily, from the less progressive and advanced countries of Europe" and who "settle first in urban 'colonies' of their own race . . . which cut the immigrant off from American influences and thus constitute a serious menace to the community"). The commission concluded that radicalism and criminality were not transient phenomena of immigration, but were inherent in several of the Roman Catholic "races," notably Italians.

The commission's work led to the passing of two federal laws that changed the complexion of America dramatically: the 1921 Emergency Quota Act and the 1924 Immigration Act, which for the first time set restrictions on immigration by national origin. These acts banned immigration from Asia and Africa and dramatically reduced the number of Italians and Jews allowed into the United States. The number of Italians fell from 200,000 in 1910 to only 4,000 after 1924. Yet the fears continued unabated, and in the next decades they were amplified by the increasing violence of the wider world. Between the lethal Italian-immigrant terrorist wave that included scores of bomb attacks against politicians and businesspeople in 1919 and the large-scale bombing of Wall Street in 1920, the rising spectre of fascism across Catholic Europe, and increased Catholic lobbying for government funding of separate parochial schools, Americans in the decades before the Second World War looked at their Catholic neighbours with even more suspicion—in much the same way that the combination of al Qaeda terrorism, rising Islamist politics abroad and sharia tribunals at home would later cause them to look askance at Muslim neighbours.

Fear of Catholic immigration did not abate after the war. The religious and political affinities of Catholics had fallen under deep suspicion, and they were often seen as representatives of an alien and hostile civilization—not just by Blanshard and his ilk, but by much of the intellectual community. The sociologist Theodor Adorno drew wide support in North America by concluding that Nazism had been rooted in the Catholic cultures of southern Germany. Following his lead, the American sociologist Seymour Martin Lipset argued that the strong Catholic backing for Senator Joseph McCarthy's anticommunist witch hunts was proof that Catholics were naturally susceptible to despotism. The social psychologist David McClelland built a career discovering that Catholic families produce fewer children with "high achievement potential," which he used to explain the relative poverty of Italy, Spain and Ireland compared with Britain and Norway. As a result, by the time Blanshard's call for mass anti-Catholic activism was published in 1949, it seemed commonsensical to many American, Canadian and British citizens that Catholic immigration posed a grave threat.[11]

Throughout the 1950s, scholars and journalists earnestly discussed the possibility that the combination of Catholic disloyalty, a new wave of Catholic immigration and ultrahigh Catholic birth rates could lead to the election of a Catholic president who would impose religious law upon the country. When Blanshard's prophecy seemed to come true—and yet didn't—with the 1961 inauguration of a Catholic president, John F. Kennedy, the entire ideology seemed to deflate. Catholic Americans, it turned out, were simply Americans. Almost overnight, the Catholic-tide hysteria vanished across the English-speaking world. After the 1960s, Protestants, Jews and Catholics were able to join hands and bide their time until they could unite in fear around the next wave of menacing outsiders.

II THE JEWISH TIDE

JEWS HAVE FACED HATRED and distrust in Western countries for thousands of years, and since the twelfth century have suffered periodic bouts of ghettoization, expulsion and mass murder. What happened during the seven and a half decades from 1870 to 1945, however, was something new. The mass migration of millions of Jews from Eastern Europe set off loathing and fear on a scale that had never been seen before. If Jews in the West had previously been resented for their supposed success and elite status—as the ultimate insiders—these new immigrants, who spoke different languages, maintained strange and conservative religious customs and seemed determined not to integrate, were denounced as total outsiders. Anti-Semitic activists seized on public suspicions and painted all Jewish believers as potential threats. In Britain and North America, the result was intolerance and exclusion, but in Central Europe it was outright hatred and murder, culminating in the Nazi Holocaust.

In the final decades of the nineteenth century, the new nationalism in Russia and the former Habsburg Empire led to pogroms and expulsions of Jews. At first they fled mainly to the capitals of Central Europe. Then, after 1885, Prussia expelled Russians and Poles (most of them Jewish) from its territory and they fled westward. Between 1881 and 1899, Jewish emigration from Eastern Europe rose from 3,000 a year to 50,000; by 1914, it was 135,000. Many moved on to Germany and France; a great many more boarded ships to escape further. By the 1890s, six ships a week were evacuating Jews from the Baltic States. The United States and Canada were often the intended destination, but a great many emigrants disembarked in Britain. By the beginning of the First World War, at least 120,000 Jews had arrived in British cities.[12]

As William Brustein notes in his history of modern European anti-Semitism, the new immigrants changed the public image of Jews. Traditional anti-Semitism had become rare in the century following the Enlightenment, as the Church lost its power of disapproval and Jews came to be accepted legally and politically. Britain even elected as prime minister Benjamin Disraeli, who was born to Jewish parents. But the "Jewish tide" created a new perception that spread quickly among gentiles and established Jews alike:

> The new Jewish immigrants who came largely from Russia and the Habsburg Empire differed in dress, language, and customs from the more assimilated Sephardic Jews. . . . It was not simply the sudden and dramatic increase in the Jewish population, but perhaps more the strange customs and appearances of the Eastern European Jews or *Ost-Juden* that affected the racial perception of Jews in the West. For the most part, these newly arrived Ashkenazic Jews from East Central Europe had come out of an isolated pre-modern civilization in which they had shown little interest in adopting the host culture. . . . The Eastern European Jews and their Western European co-religionists differed significantly. In contrast to Western European Jews, the Eastern European Jews were typically less assimilated, more predisposed toward the Yiddish language and religious orthodoxy, less likely to intermarry and maintain a low birthrate, and more likely to hold lower-middle-class or proletarian jobs and to support Zionism or socialism. . . . The depiction of the Eastern European Jews as fanatical, backward, superstitious and unenlightened emanated from both non-Jewish and Jewish quarters.[13]

In London and New York, the Jewish-immigrant neighbourhood quickly came to be seen as a parallel society, one whose appearance, customs and treatment of women seemed to have emerged from the Dark Ages. Reform and liberal Judaism, which had strong followings in cosmopolitan Western Europe, certainly wasn't known to the hundreds of thousands of newcomers, whose faith was strictly Orthodox and conservative. The new immigrants' dark clothes and head coverings soon became emblems of civilizational conflict.

In London, Robert Winder notes in his history of immigration to Britain, "the Jewish neighbourhoods swiftly evolved a striking new appearance: black hats, long hair, beards, Yiddish signs above the shops, snatches of strange (to the bewildered locals) foreign music from upstairs rooms and kosher butchers. They were, in other words, distinctive and isolated, clustered as they were around the 'hebrot'— small, independent religious societies oblivious to the wider world." The new Jews came to be associated with criminality and violence (even though there was no indication that Jewish crime rates were higher than those of any other poor neighbourhoods). Indeed, when the Jack the Ripper murders came to light in 1888, it was generally assumed among the public and in the media that "he must be one of those pitiless ruffian Jews" who had turned Whitechapel into a feared district.[14]

The *Evening Standard* published a widely read series of articles on the threat posed by the Jewish-immigrant enclaves of Whitechapel and Spitalfields. One, titled "Problem of the Alien," announced that the city was being "overrun by undesirables" who had established "vast foreign areas." Others described these dangerous, criminal neighbourhoods, laced with "the darkest and most forbidding of alleys" which "none but residents would willingly go through after dark," so great was the risk of being "attacked or molested." Jewish anarchist gangs were said to run coffee houses meant to "tempt poor flies into the trap," where the victims would be stripped of their money or radicalized. Jews were widely associated with political extremism and violence. The Russian Revolution in 1917 and the Bolshevik movements in many European countries—in some ways the period's counterpart to Islamist extremism today—were characterized in the media as Jewish-led events. The widely used term "Judeo-Bolshevism" was the period's equivalent to today's "Islamo-fascism." In Western Europe at the time, communist and anarchist extremism and terrorism were often discussed as ethnic, rather than political, phenomena. "After 1918," writes British historian Tony Kushner, "the leading spirits of High Toryism—the *Times*, the *Morning Post* and the *Spectator*—were quick to accuse Jews of being the central force behind Bolshevism and a generally malevolent world power. . . . They mainly saw Jews as aliens whose power needed to be contained."[15]

A similar phenomenon took place on an even larger scale in North America. Between the 1880s and 1914, millions of Jews immigrated to the United States; by 1917, their numbers had increased sixteenfold to 3.9 million, or 3.3% of the country's population. In contrast to the small and comparatively prosperous community of mainly German Jews who had come to the United States before then, the historian David A. Gerber writes, "the eastern Europeans were poorer upon arrival; more prone to concentrate in the immigrant slums of the major northern cities; more troubled by such social problems as poverty, desertion, and unemployment; and more likely to be pre-modern in their habits and traditional in religious matters."[16] Even though there was no evidence that Jews were more criminally inclined than native-born Americans, it was widely believed that their neighbourhoods were rife with violent criminal gangs and political extremists; the largest of them, Manhattan's Lower East Side, remained a dense, ultracrowded neighbourhood with a dangerous reputation for decades.

The police had a particular antipathy to Jews, whom they saw as naturally criminal. Historian David Reimers recounts: "In 1908 New

York City's police commissioner, Theodore A. Bingham, wrote a piece for the *North American Review*. He singled out Jews, saying that, although Jews were only one quarter of the city's population, 'half of the criminals' were Jews. He said, 'They are burglars, firebugs, pickpockets and highway robbers . . . but though all crime is their province, pocket-picking is the one to which they take most naturally.'"[17]

On top of this, academics and government officials frequently claimed that Jewish immigrants were lowering the average intelligence of the people. The 1911 report of the Dillingham Commission concluded that "63 per cent of school children with a Southern Italian background were 'retarded'—meaning two or more years behind the norm for their age groups in school—exceeded only by the children of Polish Jews, at nearly 67 percent." Psychologist Henry H. Goddard declared, after screening immigrants to the United States in the years before the First World War, that 60% of Jews, and 76% of new Jewish immigrants, were "morons."[18]

The birth rates of these immigrants were another source of deep alarm. Warned Madison Grant in his 1916 bestseller *The Passing of the Great Race*, "The native American is vanishing from much of the country . . . literally being driven off the streets of New York City by the swarms of Polish Jews." He accused native-born Americans of becoming soft, decadent and resigned to their fate. The "altruistic ideals" and "maudlin sentimentalism" of those indifferent to immigration had led to a "racial abyss" in which white Christian Americans "will become as extinct as Athenians of the age of Pericles and the Vikings of the age of Rollo."[19]

In reality, these new Jews were poor, uneducated and cloistered immigrants who were slowly but confidently integrating themselves into American life. But this didn't happen quickly or easily. In 1909, almost 26% of American Jews were illiterate, compared with 1.1% of Anglo Americans. Eventually the squalid London East End slum market stalls denounced by British newspapers and police officials would turn into Marks & Spencer and Tesco; the fried-fish street food introduced by Yiddish-speaking immigrants combined with the fried potatoes of French Huguenot refugees would become the quintessentially British fish and chips. The destitute Jews of Manhattan's Lower East Side would become leaders in academia, business and politics. But it was often two generations before Eastern European Jews were fully included in the economic, educational and political system. And until they were, their apparent backwardness led them to be condemned as a threat to civilization.

Beginning in the 1880s and right through to the Second World War, Europe and North America saw a string of bestselling books devoted to these claims. One of the earliest and most influential was *La France Juive* by the French journalist Edouard Drumont. He argued that the Jewish newcomers were loyal not to France but to their religion, which was effectively an ideology of conquest, and were attempting to impose their religious laws on the Republic.* Drumont's book, as a number of commentators have noted, is strikingly similar in tone and argument to twenty-first-century works by Robert Spencer or Bat Ye'or.

One of his German counterparts was the Catholic writer August Rohling, who published a dozen works between 1878 and 1903 that described Judaism as an ideological movement bent on world domination and governed by the Talmud, which, in his description, instructs Jews "to treat Christians as servants and permits Jews to violate Christian women and charge Christians exorbitant rates of

---

* Drumont's theories would make him the leading accuser of Captain Alfred Dreyfus in the sensational 1899 trial for treason. When Émile Zola wrote, in his "j'accuse" letter, of "the 'dirty Jew' obsession that is the scourge of our time," he was referring fundamentally to Drumont and his followers, for whom the Dreyfus Affair had been a key political moment.

interest on loans." Rohling popularized the idea of the Jew as an "enemy within."

Even more strongly influenced by Drumont was the German journalist Wilhelm Marr, who played a huge role in turning anti-Semitism from a creed limited to devout Christians into a widespread social belief. He, too, portrayed Jews as a disloyal, fast-breeding fifth column bent on imposing foreign religious laws upon the society around them. His book *Der Sieg des Judentums über das Germanentum* (The victory of the Jews over the Germans) was a major bestseller, going through 12 editions in its first year. He was careful to say, like the Muslim-tide writers a century later, that he had no animosity against individual Jews; in fact, he praised the strength of their family life and their robust religious faith, contrasting it to a weakened, exhausted German society that was at risk of being overwhelmed. The Jews, he wrote, were fundamentally incapable of assimilating into European society and were following the commands of their religion to "Jewify" the societies around them.[20]

These bestsellers soon had political repercussions. In the United States, the political movement to stop the Jewish tide was launched by the Immigration Restriction League, whose prominent backers included Harvard University president Lawrence Lowell.[21] Their lobbying was instrumental in sparking the legislative programmes that led to the immigration restrictions of the 1920s, and the widespread refusal to accept Jewish refugees before and during the Holocaust.

Facing similar popular pressure, Britain passed the Aliens Act of 1905. Even though it did not contain the word "Jew," Kushner writes, "it is clear that the major purpose of the Act was to stop the flow of East European Jews into Britain." The Aliens Act had the almost immediate effect of increasing the legitimacy of anti-Semitism, and the years from 1905 to 1914 were noted for their intensity of rhetoric and policies aimed at Jews. It also resulted, during the First

World War, in the deportation of 20,000 aliens and the internment of 32,000, including large numbers of Jews.[22]

In Germany, these popular new ideas meshed with grave social and political conditions to create history's most dangerous period of anti-Semitism. It was not inevitable that Germany would become the European centre of Jew hatred. As Brustein's analysis of the period concludes, it was the combination of "declining economic conditions, rising Eastern and Central European Jewish immigration, and the growing popularity of the revolutionary left linked to the perception of a Jewish overrepresentation on the left" that transformed anti-Semitism from a background current of bigotry before 1870 into the overt popular support for mass murder in the 1930s. By the end of 1923, Germany had experienced its first twentieth-century pogrom: three days of looting and attacks aimed at the Eastern Jewish immigrant quarters of Berlin.[23]

The image of the Jew as an impossible-to-assimilate outsider had combined with the post-1917 image of the Jew as a key backer of radicalism and violent revolution to deadly effect. In the years after the Bolshevik revolution, the *Protocols of the Elders of Zion*, that Russian-penned fabrication that portrayed Judaism as a political movement intending to take over the world, spread like a disease across the West and was seized upon by anti-Semites, including Adolf Hitler, as proof that Judaism was not so much a religion as an ideology of conquest. Those German-Jewish politicians who did hold office during this period, mainly with the Social Democrats, took great care to adhere to ultrapatriotic positions on every issue, but were nevertheless unable to escape charges of disloyalty. The supposedly Jewish leadership of violent communist movements was proffered as evidence.*

---

* In truth, while there were prominent Jewish leaders of Bolshevik movements, Jews were as much victims as perpetrators of the Russian Revolution: there were pogroms carried out by Red Army soldiers.

Brustein writes, "The disproportionate representation of Jews in the newly emerging communist movement and the spreading popularity of the *Protocols* gave impetus to the charge of a Jewish plot to sow disorder as a means to the Jewish conquest of world power." Adolf Hitler first gained attention among the right with his theory that Germany's surrender in the First World War was the result of a Jewish "stab in the back." Immigrant Jews from the East were widely seen as political threats; successive governments warned darkly of the subversive propensities of Jews from Poland and Russia.

So even as Jews increasingly became victims of violence and persecution in Germany, they were believed by much of the public to be instigators of it. The notion was absurd, of course. The Jews of Germany were, if anything, tragically quiescent. Even as they experienced the humiliation and terror of anti-Semitic laws closing in around them, they rarely responded with violence. But the idea that Jews were capable of revolutionary violence had become commonplace among the public. In November 1938, Herschel Grynszpan, a Polish Jew living in Paris, responded to the news that his relatives in Hannover had been violently expelled from Germany by buying a pistol, walking into the German embassy and shooting a diplomat. The German propaganda minister Joseph Goebbels knew that this was a rare and isolated incident, but he knew just as well that party members and much of the public would be willing to believe it was part of a larger plot. So he used the shooting as a pretense to urge people onto the streets. The result was the rampage of mass killings, lootings and synagogue burnings across Germany and Austria that came to be known as Kristallnacht.

That the German public permitted these attacks to occur indicates that they had come to see Jews as aliens. Even if they did not agree with the full racial agenda of the Nazi Party, German citizens had been successfully convinced by years of literature and politics that the Jews around them were never going to be part of their community. This widespread belief helps explain why the escalating violence, up to and including the disappearance of all Jews and their mass execution in the Final Solution, occurred with so little public resistance. While the anti-immigrant narratives of Jewish-tide thinking did not cause the Holocaust, which could only have been a product of the intense ethnic-nationalist politics and racial theories of the extreme right, it did create a public atmosphere where the worst atrocities could take place with impunity, and where a majority of Western Europeans came to accept the idea that their Jewish neighbours were hostile outsiders.

WE SEE IT OVER and over again when a new group of immigrants arrives who are members of a religious minority, usually poor and ill-accustomed to the language and folkways of their new country and the workings of its economy. In response to public alarm at these strange newcomers, writers and politicians offer the same set of frightened, frightening ideas: *They are different from previous groups. They do not want to integrate. Their religion compels them to impose their values on us. Their reproduction rates will swamp us. They are disloyal and capable of violence.* The similarities between the arguments made about Catholics, Jews and Muslims are not coincidental: this is the same argument, made for the same reasons, applied to the newest and most alien-seeming group.

That said, history never repeats itself. The circumstances and context of each immigrant wave are profoundly different, and the outcome will never be exactly the same. But we should learn to recognize the pattern and to remember the long, awkward struggle for integration endured by those earlier waves, to identify the arguments that appear every time in literature, scholarship and politics, and then take care to make sure that we don't repeat those mistakes.

FOUR
WHAT WE OUGHT TO WORRY ABOUT

MUSLIM IMMIGRANTS TO EUROPE and North America are not an invading force, a political conspiracy or a demographic threat, and as we have seen, they are not that different from earlier waves of poor, religiously distinct arrivals. That should give us solace. But it should not make us complacent or satisfied with the state of the world. There are profound problems in many immigrant communities, some of them rooted in the long-standing traumas immigrants carry with them from their countries of birth.

To say that immigration poses no threat is not to say that all is well. Rather, we should turn our attention to the genuine problems and challenges of immigration, culture, religion and the progress of the world. That these challenges are not a deluge or an onslaught does not make them any less real.

THE INVENTION OF THE MUSLIM PEOPLE

WHEN THEY GOT OFF the airplane, they weren't "Muslims." They were Indians, Turks, Arabs, North Africans, Baghdadis, Persians, Nigerians, Asians; they were British subjects, German residents, Indonesian Americans, prospective Canadians of Bangladeshi descent. Islam may have been the religion of these twentieth-century arrivals, but in general their faith was just part of the background of their lives. It wasn't the way they thought of themselves, it wasn't something they sought out in others. Despite their religion's claims to universality, they felt more affinity with non-Muslim immigrants from their birthplace than they did with Muslims from other countries. And most were too busy struggling to find work and housing to think much about religion.

By the time their Western-born children came of age, however, they had become Muslims. At the beginning of the new century, that was how the world had come to describe these immigrant communities, often fearfully. For some, it had become the way they chose to describe themselves, because their religion had become their default affinity in a polarized age, the one nonshameful source of self-identification. Meanwhile, they had become more or less integrated into the economy and daily routines of their new country, more fluent in its language, broadly loyal to its institutions. Only now they were Muslims. That was their identity, their fate, and sometimes the only handhold they could grasp during the difficult climb into the centre of Western life.

ISLAM MAY DATE BACK fourteen centuries, but Muslim has only occasionally been a preferred label of self-identification. In the last two centuries, it often has been trumped by more modern identities. Until the very final years of the twentieth century, it was generally more popular for immigrants to identify themselves by their nationality (Indian, Egyptian) or their ethnicity (Turk, Arab) than by their religion. After all, Islam spanned such a wide range of cultures, races and nationalities that it sometimes seemed meaningless and irrelevant to speak of a "Muslim people."

This changed rather suddenly, beginning in 1979, when the Iranian revolution presented the possibility of Islam becoming an instrument of postcolonial rebellion and political identity. Some Muslims living under authoritarian regimes experienced a new sense of their religion as a primary, alternative identity. The revolution also gave many Westerners a new sense of Islam as a political threat. The decade that followed saw the economies of many Muslim-majority countries collapse, saw their governments shift to military dictatorships or become more corrupt, and saw ethnic movements in Lebanon and the Palestinian territories humiliated at the hands of Israel, which caused many of their adherents to switch their identity in frustration from "Arab" or "Palestinian" to "Muslim."

For a number of economic and political reasons, many of the states of the Middle East, Africa and South and East Asia were undergoing terrible economic and political setbacks during this period, and their generally authoritarian governments became international embarrassments. To be Afghan or Malaysian, Arab or Turk, was no longer a matter of pride. The lowest rates of economic growth in the world, the highest rates of despotism and corruption, and dictatorial leaders who appeared to be puppets of Moscow or Washington—together, these degrading factors made nationalism and ethnic pride feel impossible. If your ethnicity and nationality had become matters of shame, then all you had left was your religious identity. Many seized it.

By the early 1990s, when the Ayatollah Khomeini's fatwa against Salman Rushdie's *Satanic Verses* claimed its first lives and the Persian Gulf War saw Western troops entering a Muslim country, the transformation was complete. Scholar Bernard Lewis published his highly influential essay "The Roots of Muslim Rage" on the cover of the *Atlantic Monthly*, putting the phrase "the clash of civilizations" back into our vocabulary and inspiring scores of journalists and politicians to embrace the long-abandoned idea of a distinct "Muslim world" whose values and ambitions were at odds with a monolithic West. The Islamist version of this idea—the *umma*, or unified and separate Muslim world—was gaining its own small but outspoken circle of followers, some of them violent, in the stagnant and humiliated postcolonial nations of North Africa, the Middle East and Central Asia.

This happened to be the period when the first major wave of Muslim immigrants to Britain, continental Europe and North America were coming of age, often in difficult and impoverished circumstances. Before, their source of personal identity (and sometimes the cause of bigotry they faced) was their nationality, their ethnicity or their linguistic background. They had faced discrimination as "Pakis," as blacks, as Arabs or speakers of Asian languages. Now they were Muslims. That was what political parties, journalists, activists and authors were calling them, with anger or fear—or occasionally with undue reverence.

It was also, for some, the primary identity they decided to embrace, even if their parents had not. The British writer Kenan Malik was a member of antiracist movements in the 1970s, fighting with other immigrant kids to be accepted as an equal British citizen; in the late 1980s, he was surprised to find that many of his comrades had embraced Islam, some to the point of protesting against *The Satanic*

Verses. One of his friends, Sher Azam, explained to him that his fellow born-again Muslims claimed their identity not as a refusal of integration, but as an essential part of integration—a way to hold their heads up in a country that had belittled and humiliated them, and confined them to the economic and geographic margins. "Finding themselves as Muslims has made them more British, not less," Azam told him. "They're calling themselves Muslims. Not Pakistanis, not Indians, but Muslims. They are British. But they are also Muslim."

After years fighting roving gangs of "Paki bashers" and the ugly racial politics of Britain in the 1970s, some of these second-generation kids had found a way to feel a sense of ownership of their streets and neighbourhoods—centred on the mosque—and to impose their own terms on the fight. This, Malik notes, was not an inevitable effect of Muslim immigration. For almost fifty years, immigrants had struggled to *escape* being identified by their religion; only recently, often for lack of any other source of pride, has it become a badge of self-identification.[1]

Many Muslim-immigrant communities found that their previously dormant religious identity was not only a cause of discrimination, but also a comforting source of self-affirmation. In a pattern not unlike that of Catholic and Jewish immigrants before them, the idea of a single, uniform Muslim people—of a civilization—was embraced simultaneously by bigots and by believers. Just as Jews in the early twentieth century came to be viewed as a homogenous race, not just by organized anti-Semites and bigots but also by radical Jewish nationalists, the idea of a Muslim people took hold in the late twentieth century. Omar Ba, a Senegalese community leader in Belgium, described the appeal of the Muslim identity among his young neighbours to me this way: "It's the most modern, exportable, easy-to-consummate culture pack that you can have." When you no longer see any pride or value in being Senegalese, African, black or immigrant, but the people around you still won't accept you as Belgian, British or European, almost the only welcoming cultural identity that remains—at least for one prominent group of second-generation kids—is religious.

This is what we need to understand if we want to address the real problems facing Muslim-immigrant communities in the West and confront the political and economic failings in Muslim-majority countries. The retreat into a one-dimensional religious identity is not a timeless feature of Muslim societies that flows inevitably from the Koran. Rather, it is a specific personal and political response to circumstances, and it can end just as easily as it began.

II THE PROBLEM OF INTEGRATION

WHEN JAMAL ELBOUJDDAINI got off the airplane, he was a Moroccan. His father had been a peasant farmer from the desperately poor and isolated Rif region in the country's north; his family was among tens of thousands of North Africans who came to Europe in the 1970s to fill gaping job shortages in manufacturing, agriculture and low-level service industries. When the Elboujddainis arrived in the prosperous Belgian city of Antwerp, Jamal's father was unable to speak either of the country's official languages and was barely fluent in Arabic. Like most new immigrants to Europe, they moved into the low-rent neighbourhood occupied by other Moroccans from villages in Rif, Turks from villages of Anatolia and the southeast, Poles from rural Silesia and black Africans from sub-Saharan countries. Almost all of them were undergoing a cultural adjustment, learning a new language and enduring a jarring rural-to-urban transition at the same time.

Their new home, a nineteenth-century district known by its postal code as "2060," had always been a poor neighbourhood, a tight-knit dockworkers' quarters known for drinking, soft drugs and prostitution. By the 1990s, it became known as the Muslim quarter. In the pages of Eurabia bestsellers by the likes of Mark Steyn and Bruce Bawer, it is these urban neighbourhoods in Belgium, the Netherlands, Norway and Denmark, their streets filled with head-scarfed women, storefront mosques and halal butcher shops, that are most frequently offered as the nightmare examples of a putative Muslim takeover.

At first, the densely populated neighbourhood seemed almost perfectly designed for new arrivals to become Belgians. Its busy shopping street was a short walk from the train station and adjoined the city's famed diamond-merchant district. The new arrivals turned Handelstraat into a busy thoroughfare of shops, restaurants, bakeries, butcher shops and cafés that were soon drawing customers, mainly fellow Muslims, from across the region. The housing was cheap but pleasantly designed and well located; it was possible to buy a house on an immigrant's savings, and thousands did. Jamal, one of a handful of Moroccans in his high-school class in those early years, was determined to succeed, and followed the university-bound path of the white Belgian students around him. But he watched as other young Moroccans, with the full support of the school and little resistance from their parents, dropped out at 16.

School officials had pushed these students into technical-education streams from a young age, and as a result school seemed more of an indignity than a way forward. They had no idea how to make the education system work for them, and there was no agency or support group in the neighbourhood to help them. Since the economy no longer offered any industrial jobs for high-school dropouts, these young men took to the streets. Some became drug dealers; others became enamoured of what they imagined to be the values of their parents' country or embraced ascetic forms of Islam. It seemed that some of these young men were becoming less integrated than their parents.

Things had become tougher as the children of Jamal's generation came of age, in large part because people like him, the successful ones, had left the neighbourhood. Most of the first-generation Moroccans who'd excelled in school and had made money moved into other, less segregated and more middle-class districts; they often rented out their houses in 2060 to newer arrivals. The white Belgians had also left the neighbourhood or sent their kids to schools in other districts. Elboujddaini himself now runs an impressive educational support centre for immigrant families. He is one of the few successful first-generation immigrants who still live in the 2060 neighbourhood, though he, too, has sent his own kids to schools in a less segregated neighbourhood. As a result of this large-scale flight from the immigrant-district school, local classrooms eventually contained only poor, new immigrants and attracted the least ambitious teachers, who stuck kids in remedial programmes and dead-end tracks that encouraged them to drop out. "The people who can help the most in their integration process, the role models, are all gone to other neighbourhoods," Elboujddaini told me. "You have to identify with somebody, follow a path—but that's not there."

Like other poor-immigrant neighbourhoods in Europe, Elboujddaini's became the site of low-level crime and conflict. In the early 2000s, a radical right-wing party, the Flemish Bloc, staged rallies and violent confrontations outside one of the local mosques. In 2009 after a Moroccan youth was killed, there were violent demonstrations apparently fanned by an imam with extreme views. In 2011, there was a soccer riot in June after a Morocco-Algeria match, followed in August by a street fight in which the shopkeepers of Handelstraat battled to expel drug dealers from their storefronts. Then in November Anatolian and Kurdish youth of Turkish descent engaged in a violent street battle in the wake of another football match. Most of the conflict and violence was between different Muslim communities, and the victims of crime were almost all Muslim immigrants themselves. But these incidents reinforced the sense among many Europeans that Islam had arrived, bringing with it chaos and disorder. After many generations, Europeans had forgotten that Catholic and Jewish neighbourhoods had only recently been perceived the same way.

Poor-immigrant neighbourhoods often become victims of their own initial success. Too often, a lack of specialized educational resources and physical isolation in their own neighbourhoods leave the second generation trapped, without the pathway to success their parents had. Yet it's not as if this is the inevitable fate of all Muslim-immigrant neighbourhoods. Some, like Belleville in Paris, became models of successful upward mobility and cultural mixing. Others, like the East London neighbourhoods of Whitechapel and Spitalfields, passed through a period of gang violence, religious extremism and criminality, and then flowered into economic and cultural success. In the 1980s East London's Bangladeshi and Pakistani enclaves appeared almost identical to Jamal's tough Antwerp neighbourhood today. But because of careful government programmes (especially in education), easy access to small-business resources with little bureaucratic intervention, and pathways to full legal citizenship for their residents, those neighbourhoods surrounding Brick Lane have become cultural and retail magnets, and the birthplace of a new immigrant-background middle class who have strong roles in business, politics and academia. There's no reason why Antwerp's 2060 district or Berlin's struggling Turkish districts of Wedding and Kreuzberg shouldn't look the same way within a decade.

WHY DO SOME IMMIGRANT neighbourhoods produce integration success and some cause their second generation to fall into the margins?* While Muslim-tide authors and activists blame Islam itself and many governments prefer to ignore the question, the immigrants themselves are acutely aware of the forces that crush their initial ambitions.

"It's worse now, compared to when I was a child here—the lack of schools, the lack of teachers, the lack of education, the lack of

---

* I address the fine details of this question in my book *Arrival City*.

housing. . . . They're losing confidence, this generation. It feels to them like the state and the French people have turned their back on them, so they have nothing to lose," says Samia Ghali. The daughter of Algerian immigrants, Ghali is the French senator representing northern Marseille, a neighbourhood that is home to one of Europe's largest groups of North African Muslims.

Ghali has watched as the sons of her Algerian and Moroccan neighbours fell out of the economy, landing in organized crime, drugs, or occasionally fundamentalist Islam. She is angry at both France's conservatives, who blame immigration and Islam for their country's woes, and her own Socialist Party, which tends to blame the economy and dismiss law-and-order solutions. "We don't just need schools and jobs, we need tough policing, we need mandatory military service," she says. "Remember, we Algerians are the victims of this crime. We need the state to have a presence in our neighbourhood. When we have police cars and schools, our kids can start to be part of France again."

Low-rent immigrant neighbourhoods serve as an ideal bottom rung on the ladder of social mobility, and give people a good start, but by their very nature they lack a second or third rung. They are often physically isolated, without decent transportation links; they almost always have terrible schools, because the rigid, inflexible Continental education systems are ill suited to new immigrants,* and because negative incentives cause the schools in the poorest neighbourhoods to get worse over time.

"Ninety percent of these immigrants, they are not educated at

---

* The streaming of students into advanced or technical paths at an early age and the practice of holding back unsuccessful students for a year are particularly damaging to immigrant students, encouraging them to drop out. Anglo-American "team teaching" approaches, with multiple learning levels in each age-selected class, would make an important difference.

all in their home country—not even in their own language," says Elboujddaini. "They're interested in success, but they don't know anything about assimilation. They have no idea how to start on that path. And if the parents don't know how to educate their kids in a multicultural society, then those kids are going to become poor, and they're not going to fit in. My father never had any idea about my school, my friends—he had no way of knowing what I was doing outside the house. I was the one who translated the documents to buy the house. It was just luck and coincidence that I made it. The danger that my brothers and sisters and I were exposed to—we saw it all."

The second generation, in Europe especially, is sometimes falling out of mainstream Western life, and this should be a serious concern for governments. But it is clear that even if Islam is sometimes a symptom of this loss of ambition, it is not the cause. Far from being the agents of a political-theological plot to dominate Western societies, these young people (mostly male) find themselves in this position because they have no plan or plot at all. They have been forgotten or abandoned and are reaching out for the easiest means of self-empowerment at hand. Our greatest failing would be to mistake this desperation for something more threatening. These immigrants, broadly speaking, are seeking a more modern and prosperous life—something we might recognize better if we fully understood the profound changes taking place in their countries of origin.

III THE PRIVATIZATION OF RELIGION

IF YOU WERE A MUSLIM who lived in Cairo or Karachi or Dhaka in the decades before the 1950s, you were a British subject. If you lived in Tunis, Algiers or Beirut, you were a French subject; if you lived in Jakarta, your identity was Dutch. The one thing that united the Muslim world (though the idea of a Muslim world had been all but forgotten) was colonization. For the greater part of two centuries, nearly all people of Islamic faith were citizens of lands under the control of distant, mainly Western powers. Some of these citizens were loyal and content, but many were unhappy with the state of affairs.

Their unhappiness was expressed most powerfully in nationalism. When Muslims protested against British, French or Dutch imperialism, they most often did so by fighting for national independence and a national—not a religious—identity. When independence came, it was nationalist fighters, some backed by the military and others by populist or socialist movements, who took control of the postcolonial nations and imposed a strict new form of patriotism upon their subjects. This new patriotism usually involved flags, anthems, military parades and hanging a big picture of the leader in every room. It also involved violently crushing potential political opponents, who were often Islamic religious figures.

The new leaders of former colonies generally held on to power for a long time, usually without democracy. They relied on grants from Cold War superpowers and on the exploitation of natural resources to maintain the support of their people. They seized the big ideologies of the time: socialism, collectivism, modernization and later economic liberalization were all embraced and taken over by the strongman leaders, so that by the end of the twentieth century, the people of Muslim countries tended to associate these ideas, as well as the general concept of secularism, with their dictators.

These leaders also swept ethnic identities under the rug. For instance, in the 1950s and '60s, Egyptian president Gamal Abdel Nasser, with the faltering support of other Arab autocrats, pushed for a pan-Arabist federation spanning the Arab-majority states of North Africa and the Middle East. But this federation's palpable disorder and corruption, and its military defeat at the hands of Israel in 1967, discredited the whole idea and turned many citizens away from their ethnic Arab identities.

If you lived in Cairo at the beginning of the twenty-first century, the words "liberal," "Western," "market" and "secular"—which had been repeated endlessly by the men whose pictures were on every wall—were sources of rage. The postcolonial leaders of Egypt, along with the two dozen other countries in the region, had kept their people in a retarded limbo of half-development for three generations. Despite a wealth of resources, the Arab states saw an economic growth rate of 0.5% a year between 1980 and 2004, the worst rate of any region in the world. A fifth of their citizens lived in extreme poverty, surviving on family incomes of less than $2 a day.[2]

One of the few forms of dissent that had not been thoroughly discredited and turned into a source of shame, as nationalist and ethnic movements had been, was religious. The Muslim Brotherhood and its religious-conservative offspring had been so thoroughly attacked, dismantled, banished, imprisoned, tortured and outlawed by postcolonial regimes that they were almost the only forces to have escaped the taint of corruption. On top of this, they had often been the only providers of welfare, schools and health clinics in the slums that were home to millions in the Muslim developing world. So when Arab voters, after the great uprisings of 2011, flocked to the polls to elect Islamist and Salafist parties, they weren't expressing a return to the values of a previous century but reaching out to the most credible, reliable voice of modernization and inclusion they could see.

Something profound is taking place beneath the surface of these religious-political dramas. The dominant force in most Muslim countries today is not Islamic belief but rather the modernization and detraditionalization of family and personal life. This is no less true in countries governed by Islamists. Over the past twenty years, the world's largest Muslim populations have undergone all the personal and behavioural transformations associated with the Enlightenment in Europe. They have seen an ultrarapid demographic transition—remember that Iran has gone from an average 7 children per family to 1.7—at the same time as a mass urbanization, an increase in literacy and education (especially of women) and a shift to later marriage for women (now at age 28 in Iran, compared with 13 in 1979). Behind this is a new culture, found even among the very poor, based on individualism. Personal life, even for devout believers, is no longer as likely to be silently controlled by religious traditions, but is increasingly governed by individualism and personal choice. People are choosing religion as something to invoke personally or politically because it is no longer so all-encompassing that it determines every aspect of their lives.

The Islam scholar Olivier Roy calls this worldwide phenomenon the "deculturation" of religion: faith is no longer the sole guiding force in the culture but merely a personal identifier and a political choice. Religion may become more conservative and assertive, but it is no longer universal or beyond questioning. "Fundamentalism and individualization can go together, which explains why a democratic movement can surge amid a wave of 're-Islamization,'" he writes. "It is the new primacy of the individual, not a liberal theological reformation that allows the new generation to combine faith and democracy."[3] If the Muslim Brotherhood leaders often seem similar to such American Christian politicians as Rick Santorum and Newt Gingrich, the comparison is more than facile: they are each part of a movement away from faith as an all-controlling social force into faith as a political choice, part of a culturally conservative movement amid a range of other political choices.

"Attempts to politicize religion in this way always end up secularizing it," Roy writes, "because it becomes mixed up with day-to-day politics and because it presupposes both allegiance from each person and individual freedom. Political religion is quite simply torn between two imperatives: non-belief is unthinkable, but faith can only be individual; a collective faith is therefore inconceivable, whereas previously there had been a collective system of norms. This political religion works on the principle that everyone must be a believer, but it cannot guarantee this belief, and must therefore impose a conformity reduced to appearances, which makes it impossible for it subsequently to present itself as the expression of a faith shared by an entire community. . . . Secularism engenders religion. We are not witnessing a religious comeback, but a transformation. This transformation is probably only temporary: it will not necessarily lead to a new religious age."[4] Much like the fundamentalist Christian politics of the United States, Islamic religious politics is something that comes and goes, or becomes more intense during a transition to something else. But it is no longer an inevitable or defining aspect of the society around it.

The Islamist parties that are gaining power are not a reversal of this new individualism, but rather a product of it. When Islam was an unquestioned guiding force in family and social life, Islamist parties would have been unimaginable and unnecessary. They only emerged as a response to Islam's shift into the marketplace of ideas. For the first time, Islam was something you *chose*, and that allowed it to become a political option. The price was that it became only one among many political options. "The fundamental contradiction of Islamism," French demographers Youssef Courbage and Emmanuel Todd write in their important study of the modernization of Muslim societies, "is that its leaders think of themselves as guardians of a tradition, whereas the popular wave behind them is the result of a modernizing mental revolution. Political victory is inevitably followed by cultural defeat."[5] By forcing its way into the contingent and compromised world of politics, in other words, Islam can never again be seen as inevitable and unquestionable.

Countries that already have religious governments are witnessing a "privatization of religion": its shift from being the sole governing force in society to being something that is deliberately chosen and invoked by its believers as a source of identity, but that isn't the main thing they use to make personal or political choices. Even as people in these countries identify themselves as Muslim, they no longer see Islam as the principal guiding force in their world. In Turkey, a decade of rule by a party of religious believers that some consider Islamist has been accompanied by a profound change in public belief, according to large-scale studies conducted by the Turkish Economic and Social Studies Foundation.[6] While those who see themselves as "Muslim first and Turkish second" rose from 36% of the population in 1999 to 45% in 2006, those who say they "never want to live in an Islamic state" rose from 58% to 76% at the same time, and the popularity of public religious displays such as the headscarf declined. Iran has seen an even more dramatic shift: large-scale studies by Amir Nikpey and Farhad Khosrokhvar found that Iranians in Tehran and the holy city of Qom have become deeply opposed to religious politics and the idea of an Islamic state, and view religion as a matter of personal expression.[7]

Also, the Islamist moment in the Arab world seems to have brought about a sharp decline in support for violent jihadist radicalism of the al Qaeda variety, because the same middle-class Muslims who turned to jihadist politics as a response to the repression of Islamist politics were eager to return to the mainstream political sphere. A poll by the Pew Research Center taken in the autumn of 2011 showed that admiration for Osama bin Laden as a folk hero had plummeted across the Middle East in the wake of the Arab uprisings, dropping by 40% in Jordan and the Palestinian territories and by a fifth in Egypt. Former jihadist radicals told me that democracy had turned them against violence.

I spoke in September 2011 with Usama Rushdy, an Egyptian ex-jihadist (he was a founder of the group that killed Egyptian president Anwar Sadat). "When you were [politically] blocked, as we were in Egypt, you develop an attitude," he said. "You feel that your only useful means are violence, and that your enemies are those who are supporting the regime that is killing you."[8] The jihadists, up to and including the 9/11 attackers, were never seeking to impose Islam on other lands. Rather, their goal was to remove non-Islamic forces and influences from what they believed to be "the Islamic world," so that it could become pure. They are now free to fight for that purity in the electoral arena, and they will have to maintain the support of voters who expect better lives, not just declarations of piety.

While these Islamist parties are clearly a less violent option and reflect a transient political moment, they are neither benign nor to be celebrated. They represent reactionary, repressive, intolerant and anti-Semitic forces at a moment when the countries of the Middle East and North Africa are badly in need of the opposite. We should not wish such parties upon anyone. But they are not evidence of a conquering Islam, any more than an evangelical Christian Republican president being elected in the United States in 2000 meant that Christianity was on the march—or that American immigrants could not be trusted.

Muslims in Arab states are currently voting for conservative parties. But they are also electing in increasing numbers to use birth control, to slip the tight grasp of the extended family, to educate their daughters, to engage in the more liberal forms of culture and communications, and to insist upon elections. These are the important transformations; conservative parties are just a symptom. "Westerners would like to forget that their demographic transitions were also strewn with many disturbances and a good deal of violence," the French demographers write. "The convulsions we now see taking place in the Muslim world can be understood not as manifestations of a radical otherness, but rather as the classic symptoms of a disorientation characteristic of periods of transition. . . . What the historical law associating religious crisis with fertility decline strongly suggests is that Islamism is a moment and not the end of history and that what is discernible on the horizon thereafter is the almost certain eventual development of a de-Islamized Muslim world, as there is already a de-Christianized Christian world and a Buddhist counterpart. Fundamentalism is only a transitory aspect of the weakening of religious belief."[9]

The cultures of the Middle East's Muslim-majority countries, after being trapped in economic stagnation and political authoritarianism for generations, are now rapidly transforming, propelled by a wave of modernization that was long delayed but could not ultimately be prevented. The immediate political results of this cultural transformation will not necessarily be beneficial or stable; they may produce a defensive politics of identity that could last for years. But they do show that Muslim societies are not changeless places, their behaviours and practices governed by ancient religious traditions. They are in flux. Their destinies are now controlled by the competing choices of a hundred million individuals rather than by dictators. And if the cultures of these home countries can change so dramatically and so constantly, then the immigrants they produce cannot be characterized as agents importing a changeless and alien culture—unless we force them into this role.

IV ESCAPING THE PRISON HOUSE OF CULTURE

A WORD THAT OFTEN comes up in the argument about Muslim immigrants is "multiculturalism." Anders Breivik declared he was at war against multiculturalism. In 2012 he told the Norwegian court that the children and teens he killed were "legitimate targets" because they were "political activists who choose to fight for multiculturalism." Chancellor Angela Merkel declared that multiculturalism was her country's real problem. Because Germany had failed to give citizenship to its ethnic Turks for forty years, she declared in 2010, it showed that "the multikulti concept" and the notion of "side-by-side" living "has failed, utterly failed." In 2011 British prime minister David Cameron also said that multiculturalism has failed. "Under the doctrine of state multiculturalism," he said, "we have encouraged different cultures to live separate lives, apart from each other and apart from the mainstream. We've failed to provide a vision of society to which they feel they want to belong. We've even tolerated these segregated communities behaving in ways that run completely counter to our values."

Given these condemnations, you would think that multiculturalism—whatever exactly it means—must be something that has been sought by Muslim immigrants and their supporters and opposed by the societies around them. Yet the concept of multiculturalism, if you define it as the encouragement of parallel, distinct and unchanging cultures within one nation, has only ever been applied as policy in two or three countries for very short periods of time, and it has had very little support among immigrants. In fact, a great many immigrant groups are ardently opposed to multiculturalism, notably Muslims, many of whom are fleeing the strictures of a home culture or are not interested in being homogenized into a single synthetic "community" with Muslims of other cultures. Indonesians and Arabs have almost nothing in common beyond the mosque; studies of immigrant affinities have found that Muslim immigrants from the Indian subcontinent, for example, prefer to associate with Hindus and Sikhs from "home" rather than with, say, Arab or Turkish Muslims. For every immigrant who finds a common identity in religion, there are as many who feel constrained by it. As we've seen, most Muslim immigrants have a strong desire to become fully accepted participants in the institutions of their new country. "Multiculturalism" often sounds to such people like an invitation to a second-class identity.

In most Western countries, it is easier to find Muslim commentators denouncing multiculturalism than supporting it.* The British Muslim writer Yasmin Alibhai-Brown, in her book-length condemnation of multiculturalism (which was practised as policy in the United Kingdom, to some degree, in the 1970s and '80s), spoke for many immigrants when she wrote that such policies "take differences as essentialist and never-changing, and seek to divide people into separate and mutually exclusive categories which do not reflect either the complexities of our identities or the ways in which we must all interact deeply with each other in our shared society." In short, she warns, multiculturalism "tends to fossilize the idea of culture," encouraging communities to preserve the most conservative and religious practices at the very moment when those practices would be disappearing

---

* A lone exception is Canada, where polls repeatedly show that the idea of multiculturalism remains popular among a majority of immigrants *and* a strong majority of the non-immigrant population—partly because Canadians widely identify as a "nation of immigrants" and also because multiculturalism is uniquely seen by many as a less restrictive alternative to the French-English biculturalism that had previously dominated the country's politics.

if individual immigrants were left to their own devices.[10] Kenan Malik goes even further, arguing that some of his fellow British Muslims were actually radicalized by British policies that promoted the self-administration of ethnic "communities," often by financing mosque-based leadership of diverse Muslim groups. Those policies, he argues, "helped build a culture of grievance in which being offended has become a badge of identity, cleared a space for radical Islamists to flourish, and made secular and progressive arguments less sayable, particularly within Muslim communities."[11]

There is very little appetite for multiculturalism among immigrants, and none at all among governments today. Yet criticism of multiculturalism has never been more acute; it has become part of the rhetoric of conservative parties in almost every Western country. Of course, that's partly because the term has no clear definition. For some citizens, it refers not to government policies but to the clustering of immigrants of similar backgrounds in ethnically homogenous neighbourhoods. But, as the research cited in this book has shown, this clustering is a transient phenomenon born of necessity, not the result of a desire to form isolated parallel societies. By some measures, however, those immigrants who form urban ethnic enclaves (or "arrival cities," as I have called them) often become integrated more quickly and successfully than those who don't.

In many instances, though, the word "multiculturalism" has nothing to do with culture. Rather, it is invoked out of fear of an alien religion, even if practitioners of that religion have become fully acculturated in their new country. Minarets and headscarves are, to many people, the only elements of culture that matter, and the mere presence of these things is considered the definition of multiculturalism. This is often the case even if those minarets are harmoniously interspersed with synagogues, Orthodox crosses or Hindu and Buddhist houses of worship. Indeed, this fear of Muslim difference appears to be most acute in countries that have histori-cally been defined by conflict and accommodation between multiple religions within their borders, including Germany, Britain, France and the United States. The underlying fear is not that yet another religion is being added to the mix, but that this particular religion is bringing a completely different and incompatible type of morality into the country. But of course the presence of multiple religions is not multiculturalism—it is spiritual pluralism. It does not imply any rejection of the culture or morality of the host country, and can easily take place within a single more or less unified culture, as it does in most Western countries.

MUCH AS IMMIGRANTS DON'T want to be ghettoized in parallel societies, they also have no interest in being assimilated into a homogenous, frozen "Western" cultural identity—especially in modern, urban countries where the non-immigrant population is constantly reinventing its own culture without any such instructions from above. Children of immigrants almost universally want to learn the language of their new country, participate in its democratic and educational institutions, and have a place in its economy. But there is no reason to expect that they will completely abandon their ties to their original country, their food and their celebrations, their ethnic self-identity or their religious faith. These ties will generally become less intense, blending with the practices of the new country (as we have seen, Muslims in the West tend to become about as religiously observant as the Christians around them), but they will never com-pletely disappear. The Catholic and Ashkenazic Jewish immigrants who spread westward in the twentieth century spent two or three generations in intensely religious, cloistered, educationally and geo-graphically segregated communities before gradually blending into the larger population. A few, such as Orthodox Jews in Brooklyn and North London, remain cloistered and "parallel" as a matter of religious choice. But the great majority have integrated—though not utterly assimilated—into the ever-changing larger culture.

We ought to abandon the word multiculturalism, as well as the word assimilation; both terms imply the existence of a monolithic, predefined culture that one either embodies or rejects. In real life, as we experience it in our homes, streets, workplaces and schools, there is no fixed and immutable thing known as a culture, but rather a varied and shifting set of practices built around a roughly agreed on common set of values and a collection of respected institutions. If a culture needs to be defended or defined by policy, it is a good sign that it is obsolete—whether it is the ossified "Islamic culture" glorified by the conservatives and radicals among the immigrant community or the cartoonish and Christianized "Western culture" lionized by some anti-immigrant voices in North America and Europe.

Cultures can change, diversify their activities, and absorb new communities without losing their core morality. Our values and institutions are not so fragile that they will be shattered by the arrival of a few dissenting outsiders. We should have faith in the strengths and inherent virtues of our common institutions; they have been resilient and successful enough to absorb far larger and far more divergent groups of newcomers in the past. This does not mean practising a moral relativism in which anything goes. Far from it: a common, universal morality should always be the basis of an immigrant society. The tiny minority who attempt criminal practices such as genital mutilation, forced marriage or honour killing should be tried and punished under the law, much as the few Catholics who engage in dangerous practices of exorcism should be judged by the courts. Our laws are already well equipped to deal with such aberrations. Our courts, democratic institutions and governments are already robust enough to cope with whatever explosive side effects emerge from the awkward early years of immigration. Once newcomers become part of our economy and politics, the cultural part takes care of itself. If we try to force immigrants to adopt a culture—either a fictitious Muslim culture created through multiculturalism, or, as imposed by assimilation policies, a prefabricated and bureaucratically determined version of Western culture that bears no relation to the shifting and transient needs of day-to-day life—we will only damage this transition. Culture, in the end, is not a cause but an effect.

THE FEAR OF A MUSLIM TIDE is the fear of being swept away, a fear that *they* are powerful, consistent and changeless and that *we* are fragile, temporary and malleable. Yet tides come and go. The same pattern is repeated, over and over, by every wave of new, poor, alien arrivals: the clustering into self-protective communities, the poverty and social exclusion, the alienation of the second generation, the retreat into self-defensive conservatism and faith, the temptation of religious extremism and the lure of criminal gangs, the impact of violence and trouble in the home country. And then, after these awkward times have largely passed, the smaller families, the ascent in education, the rise of intermarriage, the convergence with the new country's behaviours and values, the normalization of life.

Many of us in the West have forgotten how tough it was during previous times and how difficult integration may have been for our own ancestors. We fear a tide of alien belief, and the fragility of our own beliefs, so we are too willing to believe tales of invasion and conquest, or notions of fixed and incompatible Western and Islamic cultures, or a more general danger of being outnumbered and overwhelmed. I hope I have been able to show that these fears are unfounded, and that the genuine conflicts and reversals born of this immigration, however worthy of vigilance, are the exception rather than the rule.

In examining our own recent history along with the fast-shifting cultural realities of these new immigrants, I hope we can begin to see this human tide not as a seismic and ruinous tsunami but as a regular, rhythmic movement on our shores, one we've seen before. We should remember that a tide is something that sweeps away, but it is also something that arrives periodically, stirs up the currents, and recedes, leaving a fresher version of the same landscape. Close to the shore, it may resemble a flood. From a better vantage, we realize it is not a cataclysm or a disturbance but one of the vital cycles of human life.

NOTES

ONE POPULAR FICTION

1 Anders Behring Breivik as Andrew Berwick, *2083: A European Declaration of Independence* July 22, 2011, http://bydo.ug/5w.

2 For a detailed account of Bawer's critical career, see Jeet Heer, "The Strange Career of Bruce Bawer," Sans Everything, August 10, 2011, http://bydo.ug/heerbawer.

3 Cited in Matt Carr, "You Are Now Entering Eurabia," *Race & Class* 48, no. 1 (July 2006): 9.

4 See for example Alan R. Taylor, "The Euro-Arab Dialogue: Quest for an Interregional Partnership," *Middle East Journal* 32, no. 4 (October 1, 1978): 429–43.

5 Bernard Lewis, "The New Anti-Semitism," *The American Scholar* 75, no. 1 (Winter 2006): 25–36.

6 "The Return of Islam to Europe: Bat Ye'or Interviewed by Paul Giniewski," *Midstream*, February/March 1994.

7 Doug Saunders, "The Scary World of Geert Wilders," *Globe and Mail*, March 5, 2010.

8 For a detailed analysis of Germany's experience of Turkish immigration and integration, see chapter 8 of my book *Arrival City: The Final Migration and Our Next World* (Toronto: Alfred A. Knopf Canada, 2010).

9 Wajahat Ali et al., *Fear, Inc.: The Roots of the Islamophobia Network in America* (Washington, DC: Center for American Progress, 2011), http://www.americanprogress.org/issues/2011/08/pdf/islamophobia.pdf.

10 Spencer Ackerman, "FBI 'Islam 101' Guide Depicted Muslims as 7th-Century Simpletons," *Wired*, July 27, 2011; and "FBI Teaches Agents: 'Mainstream' Muslims Are 'Violent, Radical,'" *Wired*, September 14, 2011.

11 Princeton Survey Research Associates International, *Newsweek Poll: Obama/Muslims* (August 27, 2010), http://bydo.ug/85.

TWO THE FACTS

1 D.A. Coleman and S. Dubuc, "The Fertility of Ethnic Minorities in the UK, 1960s–2006," *Population Studies* 64, no. 1 (2010): 19–41.

2 *The Future of the Global Muslim Population: Projections for 2010–2030* (Washington, DC: Pew Forum on Religion & Public Life, January 2011), 131.

3 *The Future of the Global Muslim Population: Projections for 2010–2030*.

4 *Muslim Americans: No Signs of Growth in Alienation or Support for Extremism* (Washington, DC: Pew Research Center, 2011).

5 Eric Kaufmann, *Shall the Religious Inherit the Earth? Demography and Politics in the Twenty-First Century* (Profile Books, 2010), 181–3.

6 Kristin Archick et al., *Muslims in Europe: Promoting Integration and Countering Extremism* (Washington, DC: Congressional Research Service, 2011).

7 Dudley Sirk, "Factors Affecting Moslem Natality," in *Family Planning and Population Programs*, ed. Bernard Berelson (Chicago: University of Chicago Press, 1966).

8 *The Future of the Global Muslim Population: Projections for 2010–2030*, 25.

9 J. Johnson-Hanks, "On the Politics and Practice of Muslim Fertility," *Medical Anthropology Quarterly* 20, no. 1 (2006): 12–30.

10 Youssef Courbage and Emmanuel Todd, *A Convergence of Civilizations: The Transformation of Muslim Societies around the World* (Columbia University Press, 2011); Youssef Courbage, "The Cultural

Impact of the Demographic Factor," Anna Lindh Foundation, 2010, http://bydo.ug/88.

11   The fertility of Bangladeshi women in the United Kingdom as of 2006 was calculated to be 2.97 in Coleman and Dubuc, "The Fertility of Ethnic Minorities in the UK, 1960s–2006," 22.

12   I describe the effect of urbanization on family size in detail in *Arrival City*, chapter 1.

13   Nadja Milewski, *Fertility of Immigrants: A Two-Generational Approach in Germany,* 1st ed. (New York: Springer, 2009).

14   C.F Westoff and T. Frejka, "Religiousness and Fertility among European Muslims," *Population and Development Review 33*, no. 4 (2007): 785–809.

15   "Baby Names: Thanks, Mum," *The Economist*, January 14, 2012, http://www.economist.com/node/21542749.

16   Jack Doyle, "Mohammed Is Now the Most Popular Name for Baby Boys ahead of Jack and Harry," *Daily Mail*, October 28, 2010.

17   *The Future of the Global Muslim Population: Projections for 2010–2030*, 132–33.

18   Jonathan Laurence and Justin Vaisse, *Integrating Islam: Political and Religious Challenges in Contemporary France* (Brookings Institution Press, 2006), 27–29.

19   Kamila Cygan-Rehm, "Between Here and There: Immigrant Fertility Patterns in Germany" (presented at the University of Erlangen-Nuremberg, Department of Economics, Nuremberg, 2011).

20   Milewski, *Fertility of Immigrants*.

21   See for example Emilio A. Parrado and S. Philip Morgan, "Intergenerational Fertility among Hispanic Women: New Evidence of Immigrant Assimilation," *Demography 45*, no. 3 (August 2008): 651–71.

22   Anne Goujon, "New Times, Old Beliefs: Projecting the Future Size of Religions in Austria," *Vienna Yearbook of Population Research* 2007

(2007): 237–70; *The Future of the Global Muslim Population: Projections for 2010–2030.*

23   Goujon, "New Times, Old Beliefs."

24   Coleman and Dubuc, "The Fertility of Ethnic Minorities in the UK, 1960s–2006."

25   *The Future of the Global Muslim Population: Projections for 2010–2030,* 131.

26   "Debunking a YouTube Hit," BBC, August 7, 2009, http://news.bbc.co.uk/2/hi/8189231.stm.

27   "Illegal Immigration in Canaries at 10-Year Low: Authorities," AFP, January 2, 2010.

28   M. Fix et al., *Migration and the Global Recession* (Washington, DC: Migration Policy Institute, 2009); Demetrios G. Papademetriou et al., *Migration and Immigrants Two Years after the Financial Collapse: Where Do We Stand?* (Washington, DC: Migration Policy Institute, 2010); "African Migrants Abandon the American Dream," BBC, April 6, 2011, http://www.bbc.co.uk/news/world-africa-12810828.

29   This is explained well in Andy Lamey, *Frontier Justice: The Global Refugee Crisis and What to Do about It* (Toronto: Doubleday Canada, 2011).

30   Hein de Haas, *Irregular Migration from West Africa to the Maghreb and the European Union: An Overview of Recent Trends* (International Organization for Migration, 2008).

31   *The Future of the Global Muslim Population: Projections for 2010–2030,* 134.

32   See for example Hein De Haas, "The Arab Spring and Migration," Hein De Haas, March 21, 2012, http://heindehaas.blogspot.com/2012/03/arab-spring-and-migration.html.

33   "Church Attendance by Country, World Values Survey", http://www.nationmaster.com/graph/rel_chu_att-religion-church-attendance.

34   *Religion in Europe: Trust Not Filling the Pews* (Gallup, 2004), http://bydo.ug/galluprelig.

35 Jonathan Laurence and Justin Vaisse, *Integrating Islam: Political and Religious Challenges in Contemporary France* (Brookings Institution Press, 2006), 43.

36 *Muslims in Europe: Economic Worries Top Concerns about Religious and Cultural Identity* (Washington, DC: The Pew Global Attitudes Project, 2006), 4.

37 Laurence and Vaisse, *Integrating Islam*, 76. Simple opinion surveys show that up to 20% of French Muslims claim to attend a mosque every Friday, but these government figures are based on actual attendance counts at mosques.

38 Ibid., 169.

39 *Muslim Americans: No Signs of Growth in Alienation or Support for Extremism* (Washington, DC: Pew Research Center, 2011).

40 Ibid., 83.

41 Laurence and Vaisse, *Integrating Islam*, 206.

42 *The Gallup Coexist Index 2009: A Global Study of Interfaith Relations* (Abu Dhabi: Gallup, Inc., 2009).

43 *Muslim Americans: No Signs of Growth in Alienation or Support for Extremism*, 16.

44 Office of National Statistics, cited in Steve Bruce, *Secularization* (Oxford: Oxford University Press, 2011), 207–208.

45 *The Gallup Coexist Index 2009: A Global Study of Interfaith Relations*, 21–24. Emphasis mine.

46 Max Wind-Cowie and Thomas Gregory, *A Place for Pride* (London: Demos, 2011), 39–40.

47 *Muslims in Europe: A Report on 11 EU Cities* (New York: Open Society Institute, 2009), 73.

48 Ibid., 190.

49 Sylvain Brouard and Vincent Tiberj, *Français comme les autres ? : Enquête sur les citoyens d'origine maghrébine, africaine et turque* (Presses de Sciences Po, 2005); Laurence and Vaisse, *Integrating Islam*, 46–48.

50   *French Muslims Favor Integration into French Society* (Washington, DC: Department of State, Office of Research, Opinion Analysis M-58-05, 2005).

51   Ibid.

52   Laurence and Vaisse, *Integrating Islam*, 44.

53   Klaus F. Zimmermann et al., *Study on the Social and Labour Market Integration of Ethnic Minorities*, IZA Research Reports (Institute for the Study of Labor [IZA], 2008).

54   *Muslims in Europe: A Report on 11 EU Cities*, 112.

55   Peter Kenway and Guy Palmer, *Poverty among Ethnic Groups: How and Why Does It Differ* (London: Joseph Rowntree Foundation, 2007).

56   Anthony F. Heath, Catherine Rothon, and Elina Kilpi, "The Second Generation in Western Europe: Education, Unemployment, and Occupational Attainment," *Annual Review of Sociology* 34, no. 1 (August 2008): 211–35.

57   Jeffrey G. Reitz et al., "Race, Religion, and the Social Integration of New Immigrant Minorities in Canada," *International Migration Review* 43, no. 4 (December 1, 2009): 695–726.

58   Jacob L. Vigdor, *Comparing Immigrant Assimilation in North America and Europe* (New York: Center for State and Local Leadership, May 2011), http://bydo.ug/87.

59   *Muslim Americans: A National Portrait* (Abu Dhabi: Gallup, Inc., 2011), 22–23.

60   F. Heckmann, "Education and the Integration of Migrants: Challenges for European Education Systems Arising from Immigration and Strategies for Successful Integration of Migrant Children in European Schools and Societies" (Analytical Report for EU Commission, DG Education and Culture, 2008).

61   Steffen Angenendt et al., *Muslim Integration: Challenging Conventional Wisdom in Europe and the United States* (Washington, DC: Center for Strategic and International Studies, 2007), 62.

62 Heckmann, "Education and the Integration of Migrants."

63 Laurence and Vaisse, *Integrating Islam*, 38.

64 *Muslims in Europe: A Report on 11 EU Cities*, 93.

65 Divya Sunder and Layli Uddin, "A Comparative Analysis of Bangladeshi and Pakistani Educational Attainment in London Secondary Schools," *InterActions: UCLA Journal of Education and Information Studies* 3, no. 2 (2007); *Ethnicity and Education: The Evidence on Minority Ethnic Pupils Aged 5–16* (London: Department for Education and Skills, 2006); Geoff Dench, Kate Gavron, and Michael Young, *The New East End: Kinship, Race and Conflict* (London: Profile Books, 2006).

66 Yann Algan et al., "The Economic Situation of First and Second-Generation Immigrants in France, Germany and the United Kingdom," *Economic Journal* 120, no. 542 (2010): F4–F30.

67 Maurice Crul and Liesbeth Heering, *The Position of the Turkish and Moroccan Second Generation in Amsterdam and Rotterdam: The TIES Study in the Netherlands* (Amsterdam: Amsterdam University Press, 2008).

68 *Muslims in Europe: A Report on 11 EU cities*, 94.

69 Algan et al., "The Economic Situation of First and Second-Generation Immigrants in France, Germany and the United Kingdom."

70 Christian Dustmann and Nikolaos Theodoropoulos, "Ethnic Minority Immigrants and Their Children in Britain," *Oxford Economic Papers* (March 2, 2010).

71 *Muslims in Europe: A Report on 11 EU Cities*, 119.

72 *The Gallup Coexist Index 2009: A Global Study of Interfaith Relations*, 28.

73 Brouard and Tiberj, *Français comme les autres ?*.

74 *Muslim Americans: No Signs of Growth in Alienation or Support for Extremism.*

75 Scott Helfstein, Nassir Abdullah, and Muhammad al-Obaidi, *Deadly Vanguards: A Study of al-Aq'ida's Violence against Muslims* (West

Point, NY: Combating Terrorism Center at West Point, December 2009).

76 *Muslim Americans: No Signs of Growth in Alienation or Support for Extremism.*

77 John L. Esposito and Dalia Mogahed, *Who Speaks for Islam? What a Billion Muslims Really Think* (New York: Gallup Press, 2008), 95.

78 *The Gallup Coexist Index 2009: A Global Study of Interfaith Relations,* 40–41.

79 *Muslim Americans: No Signs of Growth in Alienation or Support for Extremism,* 95.

80 Michael C. Grossman, "Is This Arbitration? Religious Tribunals, Judicial Review, and Due Process," *Columbia Law Review,* no. 107 (January 2007): 169–209.

81 Esposito and Mogahed, *Who Speaks for Islam?,* 49.

82 Julie Macfarlane, *Shari'a Law: Coming to a Courthouse Near You?: What Shari'a Really Means to American Muslims* (Detroit: ISPU, 2012).

83 Munira Mirza, Abi Senthilkumaran, and Zein Ja'Far, *Living Apart Together: British Muslims and the Paradox of Multiculturalism* (London: Policy Exchange, 2007).

84 *The Gallup Coexist Index 2009: A Global Study of Interfaith Relations,* 31–33.

85 Wajahat Ali and Matthew Duss, *Understanding Sharia Law* (Washington, DC: Center for American Progress, 2011).

86 Alan Travis, "MI5 Report Challenges Views on Terrorism in Britain," *Guardian,* August 20, 2008; Abul Taher, "The Middle-Class Terrorists: More Than 60pc of Suspects Are Well Educated and from Comfortable Backgrounds, Says Secret MI5 File," *Mail Online* (London, October 16, 2011).

87 Esposito and Mogahed, *Who Speaks for Islam?,* 98.

88 *The Gallup Coexist Index 2009: A Global Study of Interfaith Relations,* 42.

89   Jamie Bartlett, Michael King, and Jonathan Birdwell, *The Edge of Violence* (London: Demos, 2010).

90   Olivier Roy, *Al Qaeda in the West as a Youth Movement: The Power of Narrative* (Brussels: Centre for European Policy Studies, August 2008).

91   Jonathan Masters, "Radicalization and U.S. Muslims," Council on Foreign Relations, 2011, http://www.cfr.org/counterradicalization/radicalization-us-muslims/p24354.

92   Robert Lambert, *Countering Al-Qaeda in London: Police and Muslims in Partnership* (London: Hurst & Company, 2011).

93   All European terror statistics from the annual reports of Europol, www.europol.europa.eu.

94   Charles Kurzman, *Muslim-American Terrorism since 9/11: An Accounting* (Durham, NC: Triangle Center on Terrorism and Homeland Security, 2011).

95   "Radical Muslim-Americans Pose Little Threat, Study Says," *New York Times*, February 8, 2012. The study is found at http://bydo.ug/86.

96   Nissa Finney and Ludi Simpson, *Sleepwalking to Segregation? Challenging Myths about Race and Migration* (Bristol; Portland, OR: Policy Press, 2009), 109–110.

97   Charles Kurzman, David Schanzer, and Ebrahim Moosa, "Muslim American Terrorism since 9/11," *Muslim World* (July 2011): 471.

98   Marc Sageman, *Understanding Terror Networks* (University of Pennsylvania Press, 2004).

99   Taher, "The Middle-Class Terrorists."

100 Edwin Bakker, "Characteristics of Jihadi Terrorists in Europe (2001–2009)," in *Jihadi Terrorism and the Radicalisation Challenge*, 2nd ed., ed. Rik Coolsaet (Farnham, Surrey: Ashgate Publishing, 2011), 134–41.

101 This is well documented in two major works on the psychology of terrorist recruitment: John Horgan, *Walking Away from Terrorism:*

Accounts of Disengagement from Radical and Extremist Movements (Florence: Taylor & Francis, 2009); and Jerrold M. Post, *The Mind of the Terrorist: The Psychology of Terrorism from the IRA to Al-Qaeda* (New York: Macmillan, 2008).

102 Fathali M. Moghaddam, "The Staircase to Terrorism: A Psychological Exploration," *American Psychologist* 60, no. 2 (2005): 163.

103 Olivier Roy, "Al-Qaeda: A True Global Movement," in *Jihadi Terrorism and the Radicalisation Challenge*.

104 Bartlett, King, and Birdwell, *The Edge of Violence*, 15.

THREE WE'VE BEEN HERE BEFORE

1 John T. McGreevy, *Catholicism and American Freedom: A History* (New York: W.W. Norton & Company, 2004).

2 Franca Iacovetta, *Such Hardworking People: Italian Immigrants in Postwar Toronto* (Montreal and Kingston: McGill-Queen's University Press, 1992); Franca Iacovetta, "Ordering in Bulk: Canada's Postwar Immigration Policy and the Recruitment of Contract Workers from Italy," *Journal of American Ethnic History* 11, no. 1 (October 1, 1991): 50–80.

3 Paul Blanshard, *American Freedom and Catholic Power* (Boston: Beacon, 1949), 279.

4 John Palmer Gavit, *Americans by Choice* (New York: Harper, 1922).

5 Leo Lucassen, *The Immigrant Threat: The Integration of Old and New Migrants in Western Europe since 1850* (Urbana: University of Illinois Press, 2006), 22, 48.

6 Peter Schrag, *Not Fit for Our Society: Immigration and Nativism in America* (Berkeley: University of California Press, 2010).

7 McGreevy, *Catholicism and American Freedom*, 95.

8 Ibid., 92.

9 Ray Allen Billington, *The Protestant Crusade; 1800–1860: A Study of*

the Origins of American Nativism (Chicago: Quadrangle Paperbacks, 1938), 327.

10   R. Scott Appleby and John T. McGreevy, "Catholics, Muslims, and the Mosque," New York Review of Books 30 (2010).

11   McGreevy, Catholicism and American Freedom.

12   William I. Brustein, Roots of Hate: Anti-Semitism in Europe before the Holocaust (Cambridge: Cambridge University Press, 2003), 104; Ian Goldin, Geoffrey Cameron, and Meera Balarajan, Exceptional People: How Migration Shaped Our World and Will Define Our Future (Princeton: Princeton University Press, 2011).

13   Brustein, Roots of Hate, 114.

14   Robert Winder, Bloody Foreigners, New ed. (Abacus, 2005).

15   Tony Kushner, The Persistence of Prejudice: Antisemitism in British Society during the Second World War (Manchester: Manchester University Press, 1989), 79–80.

16   David A. Gerber, ed., Anti-Semitism in American History (Urbana: University of Illinois Press, 1986), 24.

17   David M. Reimers, Unwelcome Strangers: American Identity and the Turn Against Immigration, new ed. (New York: Columbia University Press, 1999).

18   Schrag, Not Fit for Our Society, 71, 80.

19   Ibid., 75.

20   Brustein, Roots of Hate, 131.

21   Leonard Dinnerstein, Antisemitism in America (New York: Oxford University Press, 1995), 44.

22   Kushner, The Persistence of Prejudice, 11.

23   Brustein, Roots of Hate, 139.

FOUR WHAT WE OUGHT TO WORRY ABOUT

1   Kenan Malik, *From Fatwa to Jihad: The Rushdie Affair and Its Legacy* (London: Atlantic Books, 2010), 29.

2   *Arab Human Development Report 2009* (New York: United Nations Development Programme, 2009).

3   Olivier Roy, "Post-Islamic Revolution," The European Institute, February 17, 2011, http://bydo.ug/roy2011.

4   Olivier Roy, *Holy Ignorance: When Religion and Culture Part Ways* (London: Hurst & Company, 2010).

5   Courbage and Todd, *A Convergence of Civilizations*.

6   Ali Çarkoğlu and Binnaz Toprak, *Religion, Society and Politics in a Changing Turkey* (Istanbul: TESEV Publications, 2007).

7   Amir Nikpey, *Politique et religion en Iran contemporain* (Paris: L'Harmattan, 2003), Farhad Khosrokhavar, "The New Religiosity in Iran," *Social Compass* 54, no. 3 (2007)

8   Doug Saunders, "Al-Qaeda's Zealots of Yesteryear Turning to Politics, Democracy," *The Globe and Mail*, May 12, 2012.

9   Courbage and Todd, *A Convergence of Civilizations*.

10   Yasmin Alibhai-Brown, *After Multicuturalism* (London: Foreign Policy Centre, 2000), 45.

11   Malik, *From Fatwa to Jihad*, 210.

ACKNOWLEDGEMENTS

This book grew out of my research into immigrant neighbourhoods, and a mounting sense that the reality of these places and their inhabitants was alarmingly out of step with the claims being made in the media and in the pages of dozens of popular books. There was very clearly a need for a counterweight—something that would plainly and briefly address the worries of many people by stating the established facts. To ensure that these facts are as comprehensive and timely as possible, I enlisted the help of a circle of researchers who are specialists in these fields. I suspect that each of them could have written a book of even greater value, and I am grateful that they gave up their time to provide me with research.

My sections on demographics began with a research essay prepared for me by the Canadian demographer Randy McDonald, who impressed me with his writings on population trends in the Demography Matters blog and spent several years guiding me to the most pertinent population research. I wrote the rest of Part Two with the brilliant research assistance of the Bay Area polymath Wajahat Ali, who agreed to interrupt his successful careers as a playwright, lawyer, foodie and journalist to dig deep into the hard facts about integration, population and radicalization. My historical research was helped considerably by Jee Yeon Lim, an Oxford graduate in Migration Studies, who spent long hours in the British Library sifting through chronicles of the last two waves of religious-minority immigration. In London, Joanne Shurvell provided some valuable research for the book's first section.

This project has been blessed with the support and very engaged assistance of two of the best book editors in North America, Anne Collins at Knopf Canada in Toronto and Andrew Miller at Pantheon in New York. They made the writing and editing process a pleasure. John Pearce, my agent, negotiated the international complexities of this project with speed and finesse. And once again the senior editors at the *Globe and Mail*, notably John Stackhouse and Craig Offman, have shown their commitment to larger perspectives and informed debate by encouraging me to pursue these topics in my columns and by granting me time to write this book while running a busy European bureau. None of this would have been at all possible, or bearable, without my lifelong partnership with Elizabeth Renzetti.

INDEX

and immigration, 56, 57
and nationalism, 150
and nationality, 150
See also postcolonial nations
communism
    Ashkenazic Jewish immigrants
        and, 4
    as ethnic, 130
    Islam and, 25
    Jews and, 134–5
contraceptives, 45
Coolsaet, Rick, 103
Courbage, Youssef, 47, 154
crime
    Eastern European Jewish immi-
        grants and, 130
    Jewish immigrants and, 129–30
    Roman Catholic immigrants and,
        124
    Roman Catholics and, 116, 117
culture
    defined, 162
    multiculturalism and, 159–61 (*see*
        also multiculturalism)
    and religion, 152–3
Czolgosz, Leon, 123

death penalty. *See* capital punishment
democracy
    British Muslims and, 70
    French Muslims and, 70
    Muslim immigrants and, 74, 84
    past European immigrants and, 84
    postcolonial nations and, 150
    Roman Catholic immigrants and,
        115, 116, 117, 124
    and violence, 155
Democratic Republic of Congo, fer-
    tility rates, 46–7

Demos, 70, 103, 110–11
Denmark
    birth rates in, 53
    Danish People's Party, 25
    fertility rates in, 59
    newspaper cartoons featuring
        Prophet Mohammed, 72, 83
    poverty in, 74
despotism, 120, 125
Dewey, John, 116, 117
dhimmitude, 15, 17
Dillingham Commission, 124–5, 131
dispute settlement
    alternative, 90
    Islamic tribunals and, 89–90
Disraeli, Benjamin, 128
divorce
    religious tribunals and, 90, 91–2
    under sharia law, 92
Dreyfus, Alfred, 132
Drumont, Edouard, *La France Juive*,
    132
Duss, Matthew, 99

Eastern European Jewish immi-
    grants, 114
    and crime, 130
    effect in West, 127
    in France, 127
    German Jewish immigrants vs.,
        130
    in Germany, 127
    poverty of, 130
    in UK, 127–30, 133–4
    See also Jewish immigrants
education
    Algerian immigrants and, 147–8
    banning of religious symbols in
        schools, 93

United States
  birth rates in, 121
  Christianity in, 65, 96–7, 99, 153,
    155
  Congressional Research Service, 43
  Constitution, 30
  Emergency Quota Act, 125
  extremism in, 32
  family size in, 43
  Federal Arbitration Act of 1925, 92
  First Amendment, 92
  homosexuality in, 66
  immigration policy, 122, 125
  and Israeli-Palestinian relations, 65
  Jewish immigrants in, 130–1, 133
  Jews in, 42
  Latin American Catholics in, 52
  Muslims in (see American
    Muslims)
  as nation of immigrants, 124
  numbers of immigrants to, 120
  numbers of Islamic terrorist
    offences in, 106
  opinions on civilian bombing in,
    86–7
  presidential campaign in, 30–2
  Protestant immigrants in, 120
  recession and immigration levels,
    56
  religion in, 65
  religious tribunals in, 92
  Roman Catholic immigrants in,
    115, 120–6
  Roman Catholic president, 126
  southern/eastern European immi-
    grants to, 120
  State Department, 71
  women in, 66–7
  See also New York

urbanization, and family size, 45,
  47, 49
Utøya island, 9–11

The Vatican Decrees (Gladstone),
  119–20
Vienna, Battle of, 11
Vigdor, Jacob, 76–7
violence
  causes of, 82–3, 104
  against civilian targets, 86–7
  democracy and, 155
  of holy books of Abrahamic reli-
    gions, 7
  irreconcilable civilizations and, 33
  Jewish immigrants and, 129–30
  Jews and, 135
  Muslim immigrants and, 146
  radical theology and, 103
  religion and, 119
  Roman Catholic immigrants and,
    118, 123
  Roman Catholics and, 116
  support for, among Muslims vs.
    general population, 87

Walker, Francis, 120–1
Wall Street bombing 1920, 125
West
  alternative dispute resolution in, 90
  decline of, 20, 21, 27, 58–60, 131,
    133
  family size in, 38
  feminization of, 22
  jihadist terrorism in, 102–3
  Muslim majority in, 38
  Muslim neighbourhoods in, 61
  Muslim population size in, 38,
    48–54